At Issue

Should Parents Be Allowed to Choose the Gender of Their Children?

Other Books in the At Issue Series:

At Issue

Should Parents Be Allowed to Choose the Gender of Their Children?

Laura K. Egendorf, Book Editor

GREENHAVEN PRESS
A part of Gale, Cengage Learning

GALE
CENGAGE Learning·

Detroit • New York • San Francisco • New Haven, Conn • Waterville, Maine • London

Christine Nasso, *Publisher*
Elizabeth Des Chenes, *Managing Editor*

© 2008 Greenhaven Press, a part of Gale, Cengage Learning.

Gale and Greenhaven Press are registered trademarks used herein under license.

For more information, contact:
Greenhaven Press
27500 Drake Rd.
Farmington Hills, MI 48331-3535
Or you can visit our Internet site at gale.cengage.com

For product information and technology assistance, contact us at

Gale Customer Support, 1-800-877-4253
For permission to use material from this text or product, submit all requests online at www.cengage.com/permissions

Further permissions questions can be emailed to permissionrequest@cengage.com

Articles in Greenhaven Press anthologies are often edited for length to meet page requirements. In addition, original titles of these works are changed to clearly present the main thesis and to explicitly indicate the author's opinion. Every effort is made to ensure that Greenhaven Press accurately reflects the original intent of the authors. Every effort has been made to trace the owners of copyrighted material.

Cover photograph reproduced by permission of © Images.com/Corbis.

LIBRARY OF CONGRESS CATALOGING-IN-PUBLICATION DATA

Should parents be allowed to choose the gender of their children? / Laura K. Egendorf, book editor.
    p. cm. -- (At issue)
Includes bibliographical references and index.
ISBN-13: 978-0-7377-4062-2 (hardcover)
ISBN-13: 978-0-7377-4063-9 (pbk.)
1. Sex preselection--Moral and ethical aspects. 2. Sex of children, Parental preferences for. I. Egendorf, Laura K., 1973-
QP279.S56 2008
174.2'8--dc22

2008004752

Printed in the United States of America
1 2 3 4 5   12 11 10 09 08

ED121

Contents

Introduction

Technology has greatly changed pregnancy, with the development of techniques such as in vitro fertilization and in utero surgeries. Advances in medical technology have made it possible for parents to not only find out the gender but also to select the gender of their child prior to in vitro fertilization. Parents can also discover whether the fetus is at risk for a gender-linked disease. Because parents may decide not to continue with a pregnancy as a result of these technologies, sex selection is both a technological and a moral issue. It is often the religious views of the parents that determine whether they continue with the pregnancy. Major religions—Christianity, Judaism, Islam, and Hinduism—have well-defined views on gender selection that help shape larger opinions on the issue.

Christian traditions oppose abortion for sex-selective purposes. It is forbidden even if a parent is using sex-selection techniques to determine whether a child might be at greater risk for a disease that typically affects one gender more than the other, such as hemophilia and Duchenne muscular dystrophy, both of which are more likely to affect boys. One reason why many Christians oppose sex selection is because they believe that those techniques turn procreation into a form of manufacturing, where parents can create exactly the type of child they want instead of leaving it up to God. Christian ethicists fear that the desire to engage in sex-selective practices indicates a disturbing attitude: These parents would not fully embrace a child of a less-preferred gender. As argued by Brent Water, the director of the Jerre L. and Mary Joy Center of Ethics and Values at the Garrett-Evangelical Theological Seminary in Evanston, Illinois: "It is at least arguable that parenthood is characterized by the unconditional rather than conditional acceptance of children, a quality that is clearly eroded by the availability of sex selection technology."

Jewish ethicists have asserted that it is acceptable to sort sperm during the in vitro process in order to prevent the implantation of a fetus with a sex-linked genetic disease, such as Tay-Sachs (which disproportionately affects Jewish males). However, parents should not use these technologies simply because of a gender preference, say Jewish ethicists. This distinction is made because many rabbis, particularly in the more traditional Orthodox and Conservative movements, believe that enabling parents to choose the precise number of boys and girls in their families runs counter to the Jewish edict to "be fruitful and multiply." According to Rabbi David Feldman, quoted in an article for the Jewish Telegraphic Agency, if the ability to choose the gender of one's child becomes more common "it is possible to imagine that couples with three, four or five children still trying for one of the opposite gender would use [gender-selection technologies]." In Feldman's view, the use of such technologies for personal rather than medical reasons would violate the biblical motive for procreation.

Islam is less restrictive than Christianity and Judaism in its views toward sex selection. As with Judaism, it is acceptable in Islam to test for sex-linked disease prior to implantation. The Islamic view is that it is preferable to refrain from implanting an embryo that might have such a disease than to abort the pregnancy later for the same reason. In addition, some Muslim scholars believe it is acceptable for parents to choose the gender of their babies. However, Saudi theologians called for a ban on such practices in November 2007. According to the Web site IslamSet, one reason for the opposition to sex selection is that some Islamic scholars believe it could lead to significant gender imbalances.

Modern Hinduism is strongly against the use of abortion for sex-selection purposes. As explained by Vasu Murti and Mary Krane Derr in the article "Abortion Is Bad Karma: Hindu

Perspectives," Hindu leaders believe that aborting a fetus—and in Hindu societies, the aborted fetus is quite often female—creates bad luck. They also observe that the religion is misguidedly used to justify the oppression of women. The authors write, "Some Hindus have noted the karmic link between the oppression of already-born women and girls and the oppression of the unborn—especially in their objections to the tremendous economic and social pressures upon Indian women to marry and to bear sons instead of daughters." However, despite these views, India, where nearly 900 million people practice Hinduism, is a nation where sex-selection abortions are a serious problem. More than one hundred thousand such abortions took place in the 1990s. The gender ratio in India is notable—eighty-nine females are born to every one hundred males, compared to the global ratio of ninety-five female births per one hundred male births. As the situation in India shows, religion does not always change how people act.

Religious views can influence how society views sex selection in general and specifically the use of abortion as a sex-selection technique. However, as the high level of sex-selection abortion (and in some cases, infanticide) in India shows, the practices of a society do not necessarily reflect religious perspectives. The issue of whether parents have the right to choose the gender of their children is one fraught with many controversies. The contributors to *At Issue: Should Parents Be Able to Choose the Gender of Their Children?* debate how sex selection affects society.

1

Sex Selection: An Overview

Leslie Doty Hollingsworth

Leslie Doty Hollingsworth is an associate professor of social work at the University of Michigan.

Prenatal sex selection has emerged as an ethical issue over the past three decades. One issue is the rise of sex-selective abortions in countries where male children are preferred, such as China and India. In the West, the technology is used to determine sex prior to the implantation of embryos at infertility clinics. These uses can lead to ethical dilemmas such as reinforcing gender bias and creating an imbalance in the sex ratio that may lead to the oppression of a particular sex.

The first "test-tube baby," produced through in vitro fertilization in Great Britain in 1978 under the supervision of Drs. Patrick C. Steptoe and Robert G. Edwards, was a forerunner of the genetics revolution. Since then, other assisted reproductive technologies (ARTs) such as donor (artificial) insemination, gamete (egg) transfer, and surrogacy have been successful. Developments in ARTs made it possible to identify the sex of a child prenatally. Typically referred to as sex determination tests but used initially in the diagnosis of sex-linked diseases, these procedures include amniocentesis, chorionic villus sampling (CVS), and ultrasound scans. In amniocentesis, a sample of amniotic fluid is extracted and analyzed. In CVS, a tiny sample of placental tissue is removed for chromosome analysis. Amniocentesis and chorionic villus sampling are generally accompanied by the ultrasound technique, a scanning procedure in which pictures of the moving fetus can be seen.

Newer developments in reproductive technologies can be understood in the context of the more recent Human Genome Project. Formed in 1990 as an international effort of the U.S. National Institutes of Health, the project's purpose is to develop knowledge regarding the genetic basis of human disease. Its ultimate goal is the elimination of disease, particularly diseases associated with the inheritance of certain genes. The project has resulted in the identification of virtually every human gene, of genes associated with particular diseases, and of genetic defects in embryos produced through in vitro fertilization.

During in vitro fertilization, multiple eggs are fertilized in a petri dish. In a procedure called a preimplantation diagnostic test, the resulting embryos can then be tested for the presence of sex-linked genetic defects by conducting a biopsy of a cell from each embryo, through which the sex of the embryo is identified. Embryos of the sex associated with the genetic disorder can be discarded, and embryos of the desired sex can be implanted. Preimplantation diagnostic tests opened the way for identifying the sex of an embryo simply for the desires of the parents. Thus, parents can request that only embryos of a certain sex be implanted during the in vitro fertilization procedure.

A second method used in the selection of the sex of children prenatally is flow cytometry, by which the 2.8 percent heavier X-bearing sperm are sorted or separated from Y-bearing sperm through a laser process, resulting in an X-enriched sperm sample for insemination from the male partner or donor. At present, however, only the heavier X-bearing sperm are separated effectively, resulting in the selection of females as the outcome in most cases. In the application of flow cytometry to 284 embryos, gender was unambiguously assigned in 90 percent of cases, with 92 percent of them being female.

Prevalent Sex Selection Procedures

Although exact numbers are not available, sex determination tests have become common during the prenatal care of women who want to know the sex of their unborn child. There is no evidence that these tests are being used in the United States as a basis for sex-selective abortions. These abortions are occurring, however, in large numbers in countries in which male children are much more valued than female children. In India, the ratio of girls to boys dropped from 962 girls born per 1,000 boys in 1981 to 927 girls per 1,000 boys in 2001, and in some parts of India, the ratio has fallen to 793 girls per 1,000 boys. Results of China's latest census indicate the birth of 116.9 boys for every 100 girls in 2000, up from 111.3 boys for every 100 girls born in 1990. In South Korea, it is reported that 115 boys are born for every 100 girls. These trends make it clear that although sex determination tests may be illegal, their use is prevalent. In fact, advertising of ultrasound procedures in India is said to be common, and ultrasound technicians in China are said to use signals to convey the sex of the fetus to a parent without breaking laws forbidding the practice. Neglect of the health and nutrition of girls and women and high rates of maternal death in childbirth have also resulted in higher proportions of males in the general population of India.

I identified on the World Wide Web several infertility treatment centers that offer flow cytometry. Because current U.S. law only regulates the safety and effectiveness of such a technology, clinics are able to offer the procedure without regulation from the U.S. Food and Drug Administration—at least until the expiration of patents currently held, which may not be until near the end of this decade. As of July 2001, 200 couples were said to have chosen the sex of their child through clinical trials at one clinic. In addition to facilities in the United States, flow cytometry is said to be available in at least two clinics in Great Britain, although numbers are not available, and the U.S. success rate is said to be higher (90 percent for girls, 73 percent for boys) compared with clinics in Great Britain. Laws in Great Britain regulate only procedures involving stored sperm, which does not generally apply to the flow cytometry procedure.

Despite reluctance by the ASRM [American Society for Reproductive Medicine] Ethics Committee to endorse preimplantation diagnostic tests for the sole purpose of selecting the sex of one's child, some infertility treatment clinics decided to offer the procedures to couples who seek gender balancing in their family and who seek the most effective methods in doing so. The clinics made the decision after the ASRM acknowledged the use of flow cytometry in cases in which a couple had a child of one sex and wanted a child of the other. Directors of these clinics believe services offered should include the most effective. In vitro fertilization is said to be nearly 100 percent effective in determining the sex of a child, compared with the 80 percent to 85 percent rate of effectiveness of flow cytometry. One clinic director reported that "thousands of healthy babies have been born following sex selection procedures."

Having methods available for parents to select the sex of their child suggests that one sex is better or more important than another.

The Ethical Dilemmas of Sex Selection

The Code of Ethics of the National Association of Social Workers (2000) is the appropriate framework in social work for considering the ethical dilemmas presented by prenatal sex selection. The Code contains several values on which are based ethical principles that guide social workers. Those that have particular relevance to prenatal sex selection are discussed in the following sections, along with their relevance to the ethical dilemmas presented.

Value. Social Justice Ethical Principle: Social Workers Challenge Social Injustice. Social workers pursue social change, particularly with and on behalf of vulnerable and oppressed individuals and groups of people. Social workers' social change efforts are focused primarily on issues of poverty, unemployment, discrimination, and other forms of social injustice. These activities seek to promote sensitivity to and knowledge about oppression and cultural and ethnic diversity. Social workers strive to ensure access to needed information, services, and resources, equality of opportunity, and meaningful participation in decision making for all people.

The ethical dilemmas associated with prenatal sex selection that have relevance to considerations of social justice include reinforcement of gender bias; the potential for creating an imbalance in the sex ratio that may lead to or perpetuate the oppression of individuals of a certain sex; implications for eugenics; inequities in access based on social and economic status; discarding of embryos; and allocation of medical resources.

Reinforcement of Gender Bias. An argument noted early by the ASRM Ethics Committee (1999) is that having methods available for parents to select the sex of their child suggests that one sex is better or more important than another. Gender bias in society is therefore perpetuated.

Potential for Gender Discrimination and Oppression. An argument against prenatal sex selection is that the practice will lead to sex ratio imbalance. From the standpoint of social exchange theory, this increases the likelihood that individuals of the less prevalent sex will have greater relationship power than the sex in greater supply. Members of the latter group may use this power inequity to oppress the less powerful group, and the less powerful group may feel forced to accept oppression in return for the reward of having a mate. Proponents of sex-selection technologies, however, make the point that negatively sex-stereotyped attitudes already operate in some families, as in situations in which a family has three girls and seeks at least one son.

A somewhat contradictory reality with regard to the perpetuation of sex stereotyping and its outcomes is beginning to occur in China. Almost 117 Chinese male children are born compared with 100 female children. That these male children are generally only-children—resulting from China's one-child policy—has led some to refer to their position as "little emperors." The birth differential has resulted in Chinese women. Chinese men have begun to complain that women are selecting only men of the highest status as mates. Societies in these circumstances are faced with finding a solution for the many men who do not have mates. China is said to be assigning young men of lesser status into police and other security jobs (that may increase the risk of loss of life), and one news writer predicted that as a result of the sex ratio differential in India, with 111 births of males to every 100 females, officials may have little incentive to resolve conflicts between India and Pakistan (where fatalities can be expected). Some have predicted that the sex ratio differential in China will result in men exerting power through forced marriages, bride trafficking, prostitution, and rape.

Eugenics and Class Issues

Implications for Eugenics. A move toward selecting the sex of one's child is reminiscent of the eugenics movement that emerged in the second half of the 19th century, giving support to the concept of the superiority of people with certain characteristics. Some worry that this technology will lead parents to seek to select other characteristics as well, such as athletic ability, intelligence, and physical prowess. One physician associated with a reproductive medicine center has already raised the question: "What's the next step? As we learn more about genetics, do we reject kids who do not have superior intelligence or who don't have the right color hair or eyes?"

Inequities in Access. Cost is expected to play a part in sex-selection technologies because the least intrusive and invasive and the most effective are generally the most expensive. One clinic estimates the cost of preimplantation genetic diagnosis during in vitro fertilization at $10,480, not including all costs. Another clinic estimates the cost of flow cytometry at $2,000. Cost considerations result in class differentials; some people will be able to afford the most expensive and effective procedures, whereas others will be able to afford only the less-effective ones or none at all. In cultures where there is a preference for male children, impoverished or less-advantaged couples may resort to less-expensive abortion or infanticide or forgo selecting the sex of their child.

Discarding of Embryos. During in vitro fertilization, production of numerous eggs is stimulated in the hope that at least some will be fertilized. Several eggs are implanted because some of them may not develop. Couples must decide about the status of the embryos not implanted (for example, embryos that are not of the desired sex). Embryos may be donated for use in stem cell research, donated to another couple, frozen and stored, or discarded. Each choice presents a dilemma for the couple. Storing embryos is only a temporary solution. Couples may not be ready to face the possibility of their embryos being successfully developed and their subsequent biological children patented by another couple. The successful thawing, implantation, and development to term of previously frozen embryos has been advertised at 45 percent. The ASRM Ethics Committee (2001) has "consistently taken the position that fertilized eggs and preimplantation embryos, while not people or moral subjects in their own right, should not be treated like any other human tissue. Rather, because of the meanings associated with their potential to implant and bring forth a new person, they deserve 'special respect'. In the context of treating infertility, reducing the transmission of genetic disease, or conducting biomedical research, affording the embryo special respect has been understood to require strong or important reasons for creating and destroying embryos." The use of embryos in stem cell research presents similar dilemmas. Controversy surrounding the discarding of embryos may also arouse the concern of abortion advocates given that the concept of embryo adoption ascribes human qualities to embryos. Finally, the availability of preimplantation diagnostic tests to identify and select the sex of embryos will likely result in increasing numbers of embryos, because the procedures have been limited to identifying embryos carrying genetic disorders and to producing embryos that may be used to correct genetic disorders in an existing child.

Allocation of Medical Resources. It has been argued that the availability of sex-selection techniques will lead physicians to direct their professional time and skills to purposes that are not medically indicated, "thereby possibly diverting medical resources from more important uses." At a time of limited numbers of physicians, allocating medical resources to an elective procedure that raises ethical concerns may be undesirable. Proponents of the procedures point out, however, that physicians practicing in nonessential medical practices is not unusual; therefore, there is no established basis for singling out the practice of prenatal sex selection for criticism. Moreover, the ASRM Ethics Committee (2001) contends that the practice of sex selection is expected to be low and to consume a limited amount of medical resources.

2

Sex Selection Is Not Ethical

Kevin Schmiesing

Kevin Schmiesing is a research fellow for the Center for Academic Research at the Acton Institute. The Acton Institute is an organization whose goal is a free and humane society.

The emergence of sex-selection technology is a troubling sign that reproduction has become commodified. If parents can choose the sex of their children, then babies will not be welcome if they have less than desirable features, such as being of the wrong gender. This situation is already happening in China and India, where sex selection through abortion has created a significant gender imbalance because most parents prefer having sons.

"It performs a much desired service. We're making people happy."

That's the way Dr. Jeffrey Steinberg, medical director of Fertility Institutes, justified the practice of embryo sex selection in a September 20 [2006] Associated Press article. In other words, as long as people want it, somebody ought to be selling it.

A survey released [in September 2006]—the first survey of its kind in the United States—found that almost half of American fertility clinics allow parents to select embryos according to sex, and nine percent of embryo screenings resulted in such selection.

China and India are already facing demographic challenges due to decades of sex selection through abortion. Males

Kevin Schmiesing, "The Baby Market," *Acton Commentary*, September 27, 2006. Reproduced by permission.

now outnumber females by significant margins. That practice, which had appeared to be taboo in the West, has now been shown to be fairly common. The abortions take place earlier in the process, and (maybe) there isn't an overwhelming preference for boys over girls, but these are non-essential differences.

Marketing Reproduction

One might be tempted to say that this is one more step toward the existence of a "baby market," by which parents pick and choose which traits they want and don't want in their child, pay the technicians their fee, and go home happy. But it can't accurately be described as one more step toward this disturbing outcome because we're already there.

Fifteen years ago, Pope John Paul II wrote, "There are important human needs which escape [the market's] logic. There are goods which by their very nature cannot and must not be bought or sold" (*Centesimus Annus*, n. 40).

The rush toward commodification of every human good, far from being forestalled by the pope's words, has continued unabated.

The idea of child as gift is under increasing stress as alternative and sometimes conflicting notions of child as right, as burden, or as consumer item compete for dominance.

When I was in graduate school a decade ago, there were ads in the college newspaper asking for egg donors. Usually, they specified the type of donor they had in mind: white, good-looking, high IQ.

In July [2006] the British Human Fertilization and Embryology Authority granted a fertility center permission to pay women for the ova they need to conduct research. Previously, researchers were dependent on donated eggs.

Fertility Is Being Exploited

These two tidbits demonstrate that the market for women's bodies now has two facets: sex and fertility. It is predictable that the pattern of the latter will follow that of the former. Women with networks of family and friends and other options for financial support will not be selling their fertility to the highest bidder, just as such women are generally not the ones selling their bodies on the streets.

The dignity of men and women is upheld by embedding sexuality within a relationship of love. When that function is instead separated out and a market created for it, opportunities for exploitation expand.

It is sounding increasingly old-fashioned, but it used to be the case that babies were conceived by acts of love between their mothers and fathers and were welcomed into the world by their parents with gratitude (or at least, in less ideal circumstances, accepted as their responsibility because the children were, after all, their own flesh and blood).

The idea of child as gift is under increasing stress as alternative and sometimes conflicting notions of child as right, as burden, or as consumer item compete for dominance.

Parents' desire for healthy, beautiful, talented children is perfectly understandable. But that urge is taken too far when children with "less desirable" features are weeded out at the embryonic stage. The implication is that a child is not worthy of love and acceptance unless he or she fits the imagined profile.

The market is a wondrous thing. There is no better instrument for the calibration of human productivity and ingenuity to human needs and wants. But its advantages turn pernicious when it encompasses human goods that should never be reduced to monetary values. The idea of a "baby market" should repulse us. That one already exists should cause us alarm.

3

Sex Selection Should Be Regulated

Emily Singer

Emily Singer is the biotechnology and life sciences editor of Technology Review, *a magazine published by the Massachusetts Institute of Technology.*

Preimplantation genetic testing should be regulated because such tests should only be used for legitimate scientific and medical purposes. Approximately 10 percent of these tests, however, are used by parents who want to determine the sex of their children for nonmedical reasons, which leads to concerns about other nonmedical testing. Furthermore, not all medical tests are equally valid, which also raises the need for consistent guidelines for doctors and infertility clinics.

A 38-year-old woman with fertility problems has three sons but wants a daughter to round out the family. She uses in vitro fertilization (IVF) to conceive and asks her doctors to transfer only female embryos; the male embryos are destroyed. Is this use of reproductive technology acceptable? What if a couple with a family history of diabetes wants to use IVF to select an embryo without a particular gene linked to diabetes risk? If afflicted family members largely have the disease under control, are the prospective parents justified in choosing in vitro fertilization so that they can bear a child with a lower chance of developing it at all?

Ethical Debates on PGD

Such questions are becoming more common as preimplantation genetic diagnosis (PGD)—testing performed after an egg is fertilized in vitro but before the resulting embryo is transferred to the womb—makes it possible for some prospective parents to select specific embryos before a pregnancy begins. Originally developed more than a decade ago to identify the relatively small number of embryos at high risk for serious or fatal genetic diseases, such as Tay-Sachs, the technology now encompasses genetic tests for a growing number of illnesses, including some that are not necessarily fatal. And these tests are available to more and more parents as the popularity of in vitro fertilization skyrockets; approximately 50,000 babies are born through IVF in the United States every year.

All this heightens the ethical concerns that have plagued PGD from the start. As more genes associated with the likelihood of disease are uncovered, the possibility of a truly preventive medicine is within the grasp of many parents. But with that possibility come risks. How well will any one test deliver on its promise of a healthy child? Will parents feel obligated to use genetic testing without adequately understanding its benefits? What kinds of genetic tests will parents want? Recent findings suggest that an increasing number of parents using IVF are choosing embryos according to sex, and it's possible to imagine them one day choosing embryos based on other nonmedical traits, such as hair color, height, or IQ.

Preimplantation genetic testing is available only to those who opt for IVF—which now generally means people with fertility problems or a family history of a fatal genetic illness. Though IVF is gaining in popularity, it remains an expensive and often difficult procedure. But the grounds for choosing it are changing: some people, for example, are now using it to select embryos without genes linked to particular cancers— even if the correlation is fairly weak. If parents increasingly choose IVF because it will offer them the opportunity to tailor their children's genetic traits, will the economic division of society become even deeper—separating those who can afford IVF (clinics in the United States generally charge between $6,000 and $16,000) from those who cannot?

"This is a potentially disruptive technology, one that can change the social structure and order," says David Adamson, president-elect of the American Society for Reproductive Medicine and director of a private fertility clinic in northern California. "It will move us toward a preventive approach to medicine and could change our approach to reproduction."

Tests are already available for genetic variants associated with a thousand conditions, including deadly childhood illnesses and adult-onset cancers, and more genes associated with disease risk are being discovered every day. Any such gene could be a target of PGD. Santiago Munné, director of Reprogenetics, a genetics laboratory headquartered in Livingston, NJ, says his lab has tested embryos for more than 150 diseases or risk genes—most recently for a gene variant known as BRCA1, which raises the risk of breast cancer.

Some ethicists say that nonmedical sex selection opens the door to other types of nonmedical testing.

Reasons for Genetic Tests

Little data yet exists on the use of preimplantation genetic tests. But late [in 2006], the Genetics and Public Policy Center at Johns Hopkins University released a report in the journal *Fertility and Sterility* presenting some of the first statistics on the use of PGD nationwide. "We wanted to get a sense of how much PGD was being done, and why," says Susannah Baruch, the center's director of reproductive genetics and lead author of the report. "Without solid data, it's difficult to analyze outcomes for PGD babies or to help prospective parents make decisions about whether to pursue PGD."

The researchers surveyed all the fertility clinics in the United States that offer IVF, asking questions about the types of preimplantation tests they administer, how they make ethical decisions, and how they think testing should be regulated. About half of those clinics responded. According to the survey, screening for chromosomal abnormalities that can lead to implantation failure or miscarriage, or for disorders linked to chromosome duplication or deletion (such as Down's syndrome), represents two-thirds of all PGD testing. Tests for genetic diseases such as cystic fibrosis account for another 12 percent. Forty-three percent of clinics said they had received requests for PGD that they felt raised ethical questions; most of these were from parents who wanted to select the sex of a child for nonmedical reasons. The survey found that this use of PGD is fairly common: almost one in ten tests was for nonmedical sex selection, a service offered by 42 percent of clinics.

Since it is the only PGD test that is often administered without medical justification, sex selection is especially contentious; some fertility clinics will not offer it, and some ethicists say that nonmedical sex selection opens the door to other types of nonmedical testing. But other people argue that biological enhancement through genetic screening is not so alarming, or at least not so different from other types of advantages that are already enjoyed by a certain privileged sector of the population. "I don't think testing for freckles or blond hair or musical aptitude is a morally bad thing to do," says Arthur Caplan, director of the Center for Bioethics at the University of Pennsylvania. "I think parents will want to do it, so I think this will expand rapidly."

Testing for medical purposes brings its own set of problems. Only a limited number of genetic variations present the kind of clear-cut case for which PGD was originally developed: the certainty of a serious or fatal disease. But what about testing for genes that merely raise the risk of a disease?

Or for genes linked to a relatively manageable disease, such as diabetes? How serious must a disease be to justify the costly and potentially risky process of IVF?

Some kind of regulation for preimplantation genetic testing is needed.

"That is a major debate in the profession," says George Annas, chair of the department of health law, bioethics, and human rights at the Boston University School of Public Health. Another problem is that parents may eventually find themselves with more information than they or their doctors know how to use. As more disease-linked gene variants are discovered—and the list is rapidly growing—parents will face so many choices that it will be difficult, if not impossible, to determine which genetic combination will produce the healthiest child.

Testing Should Be Regulated

In the United Kingdom, a government body licenses fertility labs and regulates which tests can be administered. But the United States has fewer rules; it is one of the few countries, for example, that permit nonmedical sex selection. "Today, in this country, the clinics are the gatekeepers," says Vardit Ravitsky, a bioethicist at the University of Pennsylvania. "If you have cash and can find a clinic to provide the service, you can get it, whether it's a test for Huntington's disease or sex selection."

So decisions regarding PGD are left in the hands of doctors or clinics. Professional societies provide some ethical guidelines—the American Society for Reproductive Medicine, for example, recommends against sex selection for nonmedical reasons, though it has little to say about other aspects of PGD. But voluntary guidelines regulating a profit-driven industry may not be enough to help prospective parents. "I think there will be people hyping the advantages of this, which will be just like pharmaceutical advertising today," says Caplan. "I think people will be guilted into doing this, rather than choosing it." They may also be "guilted" into testing that doesn't make good on the promise of a healthier child; most of the newly discovered genes have relatively weak correlations with disease or play small roles in complicated processes, and some may affect the body in ways that scientists don't yet fully understand.

Some kind of regulation for preimplantation genetic testing is needed, but the rules must focus not on limiting which tests a parent can choose but on making sure that clinics can scientifically justify the claims made for each test. Then parents and their doctors can begin to make informed choices. "I definitely think the government has a role to play in regulating the safety and quality of tests and in the application of tests," says Adamson. "But the final choice, once tests are considered to be scientifically legitimate, should be left up to patients and physicians."

4

Sex Selection for Nonmedical Reasons Should Be Banned in Certain Societies

Kaberi Banerjee

Kaberi Banerjee is a doctor in New Delhi, India, and a contributor to IVF.net, a global online resource for scientists involved with in vitro fertilization.

While sex selection for medical reasons is widely accepted, the use of such technology for nonmedical reasons can lead to significant problems, particularly in societies where there is a cultural preference for a certain gender. Using preimplantation genetic diagnosis (PGD) for sex selection is illegal in many countries and should be discouraged. Using this technology for nonmedical reasons will create an imbalance in the social structure in countries with a strong gender bias and could lead to an increase in crimes against women. These problems will persist unless people are educated about equality between the sexes and women are given the opportunity to succeed.

The choice of a particular sex for a baby is either made for medical or non medical reasons. The medical reason for undergoing sex selection is to select a female fetus in order to rule out X linked conditions like Duchenne Muscular Dystrophy and Haemophilia. The non medical reasons are a couple's preference of one sex over the other. This could be due to cultural/economic reasons or family balancing (the desire to have a family that includes children of both sexes). While there is virtually no moral or ethical dilemma regarding sex selection for medical reasons, sex selection for non medical reasons is highly debatable.

There are two separate social and cultural scenarios where sex selection for non medical reasons may be desired. One is a condition, mainly in the west, where there is no bias towards a particular sex and sex selection is only for family balancing. The other situation is where there is a geographical/society based preference for a particular sex. This is present in South East Asia and China where there is a strong preference for the male child.

Allowing sex selection in societies with a bias towards a particular sex is asking for trouble in the long run. Already, in some provinces of India the female-male ratio is as low as 810 females to 1000 males and in some provinces of China it is as low as 677 females to 1000 males. This will eventually irreversibly affect the social structure in these countries. As a concerned old man in a Chinese daily mentioned "Who will my grandson marry?" This will also increase crimes against women. This is already evident in the Northern states of India where crimes against women are rising. It has been reported that young girls from the eastern states of India are kidnapped and sold into marriage in the neighbouring western states where sex selection is more prevalent.

There are various means by which sex selection is performed—sperm sorting, Pre-implantation genetic diagnosis (PGD), ultrasound detection of sex of the fetus followed by termination of the fetus of the undesired sex and finally infanticide. The last two methods are criminal offences and we shall not discuss them further.

PGD for sex selection is considered advantageous over ultrasound determination of the sex and then feticide. But we cannot ignore the fact that an embryo has life and it is absolutely perfect except for the fact that it does not have the desired sex which the parents want. In this situation, the use of PGD is ethically contentious. Furthermore, the latest article in the *New England Journal of Medicine* has conclusively proven that PGD in women undergoing IVF with increased maternal age does not improve live birth rates. PGD may also reduce pregnancy rates in women undergoing IVF solely for sex determination. IVF with PGD solely for sex selection holds great risk for unwarranted gender bias, social harm and the diversion of medical resources from genuine medical need.

PGD solely for sex selection is banned in many countries. France, United Kingdom, Canada, Japan, India and Australia being some of them. Though the American Society of Reproductive Medicine has discouraged use of PGD solely for the use of sex selection, it is still not banned in the US for this purpose. Well-off foreign couples are getting around laws banning sex selection in their home countries by coming to American soil—where it's legal—for medical procedures that can give chosen sex of their child. This kind of practice is reinforcing sexism, diverting resources for actual medical needs and must be strongly discouraged.

PGD must be restricted only for identifying medical disorders.

The issue of sex preference and selection on a societal level needs to be addressed in its root. Clearly if this practice continues and has further progressed via assisted reproductive techniques the exacerbated imbalance will hugely affect many generations to come. However, once there is women empowerment and women are financially strong this gender bias will slowly erase.

Let us take for example India. India now has a woman President, a female prime minister before many western countries, and women in cities are doing professionally and financially well in fields like medicine, law, finance and journalism.

Yet women are harassed for dowry and a female child is considered a burden. If a section of society can achieve empowerment then why not all . . . Educating the masses is essential. Boys and girls have to be treated equally, incentives for women education and jobs must be enforced. This will take time . . . maybe two or three generations for the mind-set to change, but it is not impossible.

In my opinion sperm sorting for family balancing in a society where there is no preference for a particular sex is justifiable. However these couples need to know that there is a 25% chance of having a baby of the undesired sex by this method.

I would therefore conclude by saying that PGD must be restricted only for identifying medical disorders. Its indication for sex selection must be banned in societies where there is traditional gender bias for the male child. The problem must be addressed at the root and emphasis must be to bring a change in traditional mind-set.

5

Women Should Have the Right to Choose the Sex of Their Children

James Hughes

James Hughes is the executive director of the Institute for Ethics and Emerging Technologies and a professor of health policy at Trinity College in Hartford, Connecticut. The institute aims to help people understand the impact of new technologies and lessen the risks of these technological advances.

Efforts to prevent women from having abortions have strengthened in the United States and other countries. These attempts are wrong because women should have the right to choose whether they have children and what kind of children they have, including children of a particular gender. Arguments against sex-selective abortion on the basis that it will lead to gender imbalance or increased violence by single males are groundless. The best way to address issues surrounding bias toward girls and women is through government policies that improve economic and educational opportunities for girls instead of limiting a woman's control over her body.

Responding with alarm to the U.S. Supreme Court decision permitting the banning of late-term abortions reproductive rights activists have insisted that *any* restrictions on a woman's right to choose must be fought.

For instance South Carolina is considering legislation that would require pregnant women to undergo an ultrasound and

James Hughes, "Sex Selection and Women's Reproductive Rights," ieet.org, May 10, 2007. Reproduced by permission.

view images of their embryo before being permitted to have an abortion. South Carolina already has the toughest climate for abortion rights in the United States, causing the number of clinics in that state to drop from 14 to 3 in ten years, with a 50% drop in abortions. Forcing women seeking abortions to view an ultrasound would presumably deter even more women from seeking them from the dwindling number of providers.

Criminalizing Abortion Worldwide

One would think that the obvious pro-choice position would be that a woman has a right to know the contents of her womb with any test she chooses, including ultrasound, but should not be forced to have one, just as she should have the right to continue or terminate her pregnancy with or without that information. But this is far from obvious to a bioconservative minority within reproductive rights activism.

Responding to the slowly shifting sex ratios in India and China where male-biased sex selective abortion is widely practiced a global bioconservative alliance has emerged to demand harsh punishment for providers of ultrasound and abortion in those countries. Some activists would like to see sex selective abortion banned worldwide. These demands are popular across the political spectrum, since religious conservatives welcome any restriction on reproductive freedom, and progressives have contempt for the patriarchal attitudes that lead to male preference. The language of millions of "missing girls" and widespread "foeticide" has equated sex selective abortion with the murder of girls and ethnic genocide. The argument is also advanced that the changing sex ratio in those countries will have bad consequences for women and social stability.

India and China, under increasing international pressure, have stepped up the criminalization of ultrasound and abortion, as have countries such as Vietnam, South Korea and Taiwan. In India doctors can be, and are being, imprisoned for providing women ultrasound and abortion, unless they are at a high-risk of having a pregnancy with congenital anomalies.

Disability extremists have in turn seized on the unpopularity of sex selective abortion to argue that aborting feti with congenital abnormalities is a form of discrimination against the disabled, and should also be banned.

Even the humanist movement is subject to this form of bioconservative coercion, as a recent article in the IHEU [International Humanist and Ethical Union] journal on the tragedy of foeticide in India attests, insisting that the restrictions on reproductive choice be enforced with no mention of reproductive rights.

Women Have the Right to Choose Their Children

Briefly, then, I want to recapitulate the arguments for women having the right to choose what kind of child they have, including its gender, whether they live in the affluent North or India or China.

First, however, I feel obliged to point out that I had no preference for boys or girls when my kids were feti, and I have contempt for the patriarchal attitudes that lead to boy preference. But people bring all kinds of attitudes that I dislike to their reproductive decision-making, and the question is whether our disdain for a patriarchal prejudice warrants contravening women's reproductive liberty.

Few parents in the developed world express any interest in using sex selection, and the majority of those who do want to use it want it to 'balance' their families.

One of the more disingenuous aspects of the debate about sex selection is that very few of the activists in the North demanding bans on sex selection in the developing world promote such bans in their home countries where they would be far less popular. Insofar as their arguments hinge on the alleged harm done to the unconditional love of parents for children when parents make choices about the kind of children they have, this would apply equally to Americans or Germans choosing their children's genders.

This argument for "unconditional love" leads naturally to questioning the ethics of contraception, however, which only Catholics do; if unconditional love of parents requires accepting without question whatever God sends your way, then you shouldn't choose how many kids to have either. Parents who use contraception, sex selection or any fertility regulating technology are alleged, by this argument, to devalue all their children into commodities. In fact, the research has consistently shown that "children of choice" produced through fertility treatments are as or more loved than the children produced by the usual methods which require far less commitment and forethought.

Gender Preference Is Not an Issue

Bans on gender selection have little other rationale in the developed North, since research on gender preference in developed countries, Europe and North America, show only a slight gender preference if any. (Gender preference in Japan actually favors girls three-to-one, although it is rarely practiced there.) Few parents in the developed world express any interest in using sex selection, and the majority of those who do want to use it want it to "balance" their families, to have both a daughter and son in the family. Consequently the overall effect on gender balance in the developed world would barely dent the 51%/49% female-to-male ratio which currently makes it harder for *women* to find mates.

If it is in fact the obligation of the state to ensure that there is a perfect 50/50 gender balance—so that every man and woman in society can find someone of the opposite gender—then male preference sex selection should in fact be state policy in the developed North until we achieve such a balance. As much as some of us would like to have been able to insist that the federal government had an obligation to make sure we found a sex partner I don't really think that is a state obligation.

Society Will Adapt

The demand for a ban on sex selection thus suggests yet another serious bit of doublethink for progressives: it is based on normative ideas about sexuality and family that progressives have otherwise tried hard to critique and discard. Not every man wants or needs a woman, and not every woman needs or wants a man. If there are fewer women than men, or vice versa, it will be irrelevant for some, and others will adapt. Individual reproductive expectations, and sexual desires and identities can and do adapt to availability. The evidence is clear that sexual preference is only in part biologically determined, and that situational factors play some role. Many men become "situationally gay" in boys' schools, prisons or the military. In the developed world growing numbers of people are bisexual, remaining single or forming alternative family structures, and in a world with hooking-up, polyamory [having more than one romantic relationship at a time] and virtual sex, those who can't find a single person of the opposite sex to form a long-term monogamous bond with have plenty of alternatives. Polyandry, one wife with several husbands, has been practiced by Tibetans and other societies, and could be re-introduced. Openness to gay sex, porn and non-marital sex are also growing rapidly in the developing world, to the consternation of religious and neo-Maoist Puritans.

Another reactionary strategem of the opponents of sex selection in the developing world is the reification of the unattached male as a violent rapist and criminal, a "surplus male," as exemplified in [Andrea] den Boer and [Valerie] Hudson's 2004 book *Bare Branches: The Security Implications of Asia's*

Surplus Male Population. It is of course true that areas with more young men than young women, like the early American West, have a higher crime rate, and that marriage and family has a stabilizing effect on male risk-taking. (It is equally true that there is a high rate of violence in poor African-American neighborhoods that have a skewed female-to-male ratio in favor of females.)

Governments should and are changing the economic incentives that lead to male preference in abortion.

But it is quite extraordinary for purported progressives to argue that women should be denied reproductive choice in order to ensure that there are enough girls in the next generation to marry and pacify violent males. Why not propose instead that males be taught non-violent conflict resolution and punished harshly for rape? Would male predominant societies really go to war to kill their excess males and bring home brides as booty? If removing women's reproductive freedom were the only method to prevent such a dystopian future it might be warranted, but fortunately there are many alternative policies to address "surplus males" from international peace-keeping, to male emigration and female immigration, to male behavior modification.

Most directly governments should and are changing the economic incentives that lead to male preference in abortion. In 2003 the Indian government began to give homeless women with girls twice as much welfare assistance as women with boys, and legislation is pending in the Lok Sabha to provide free medical and education assistance to all of India's girls, contingent on their attending school and remaining single to the age of 18. China is offering parents with one or two girls old age pensions as a selective incentive to have girls.

Actually, providing universal old age security would probably be even more effective at eliminating boy preference. A major source of parental desire for sons is the weakness of social welfare provision for senior citizens, and the far greater likelihood that a son will have income to provide for his parents. Expanding educational and employment opportunities for girls, and providing a state pension system, would go a long way to reduce male gender preference.

Another argument propounded against sex selection is that male preference sex selection reduces women's political influence in society by reducing their number, which is of course true. But it does not follow that their rights are any less likely to be respected if they are 45% of the population than if they are 51%. Many minorities have fought for and won rights from majorities in the developed North, as well as in the developing world, from India's scheduled castes to non-Han Chinese. Civil rights do not and should not depend on population proportion. The logic of that argument would be that we should advance the rights of the disabled, GLBT [gay, lesbian, bisexual, and transgendered], or an ethnic group by working to increase their proportion in the population. That's bad social science and worse public policy. The defense of women's rights begins with the defense of their right to control their own bodies, not from their proportion in the population. Securing women's reproductive rights today is essential for ensuring their rights in 2025.

The Problem of Feminist Doublethink

Pro-choice opponents of sex selection again display their doublethink when they use terms like "missing girls" and "foeticide." As Catholics and other opponents of reproductive freedom rightly point out, why is it foeticide only when the fetus is a girl? If there is a two-to-one ratio of aborting female feti to aborting male feti in India, leading to tens of millions of "missing girls" doesn't that mean there are millions of "missing boys" as well? Reproductive rights are weakened every time an opponent of sex selection argues as if aborting a female fetus is equivalent to the murder of a girl person. It is not.

Most shocking about the feminist doublethink on the issue is the substantial harms to girls that banning sex selection imposes. Patriarchal societies have routinely abused, malnourished and murdered unwanted girls. Child and infant mortality for girls remains far higher than for boys in India and China. Giving mothers a choice about whether to bring a girl or a boy into their family reduces the likelihood that girls will be born into families that see them as unwanted second-class citizens. If all those "missing girls" had been born into families that didn't want them, millions of them would have suffered as a consequence. . . .

Another problem with the doublethink around sex selective abortion is that it dismisses or underestimates the potentially positive impacts on the status of women that the changing gender ratio is having in China and India. There is little empirical work on these effects yet, but many anecdotal reports suggest that one immediate benefit of the changed gender ratio is that women who would otherwise be considered unmarriageable are now able to find partners. This includes disabled women, older women, widows, women who want higher education and careers, and women of otherwise undesirable religious, ethnic and caste backgrounds. As desperate men relax their expectations about what kind of bride is acceptable, and women become more socially mobile, this will increase the options for all women in sex ratio-shifted societies.

Another change in India has been the relaxation and even reversal of the expected bridal dowry in India. Now would-be bridegrooms are either dropping any expectation of receiving a dowry, or offering a dowry to the bride's family. While this change has been luridly described in the press as the growth of bride selling, the reporting ignores the fact that tens of thousands of Indian wives were murdered in the 1980s and 1990s because their husband's family wanted to collect a second dowry. Removing the bridal dowry not only protects wives from murderous in-laws, and improves their choices in the marriage market, but reduces the dowry-burden incentives that cause families to prefer sons over daughters in the first place.

A third beneficial consequence of the changing sex ratio has been state policy to encourage families to have girls, such as the subsidies for girls in India and experiments with free university tuition for girls in China. Affirmative action policies ensuring equal number of boys and girls in higher education and employment would also benefit women in a sex ratio-effected society.

Finally, the case against sex selection takes no account of the advance of fertility technology, which will allow gender selection earlier in the pregnancy and even before conception. Blood tests now enable sex determination as early as six weeks, and sperm-sorting with in-vitro fertilization allows pre-conceptive sex selection. Eventually there will be a pharmaceutical or contraceptive device which will allow parents to choose to only conceive embryos of the desired sex without recourse to abortion or in-vitro fertilization. Will the opponents of sex selection argue that these should also be outlawed?

Restricting Reproductive Freedom Harms Women

In conclusion, a woman's right to know the contents of her own body, and to make a choice about whether to continue her pregnancy or not, should be defended against laws trying to stop prenatal sex selection, either in the developing world or in the developed world. Restrictions on women's reproductive freedom harm the interests of women and girls, and ignore myriad social policy solutions, such as education and income incentives to have girls and universal old age pensions, that provide better answers to the strains of unbalanced sex ratios. The opponents of sex selection trumpet all accounts of increased discrimination against women resulting from unequal sex ratios while ignoring growing evidence of positive cultural change and women's empowerment from women's enhanced marriage prospects. Opponents of sex selection reify a conservative heteronormative model of sexuality, gender roles and family structure, while arguing that unmarried men are social time bombs who can only be controlled by a wife. Eventually the social policy dilemma around sex selection will presumably be made moot since would-be parents will be able to use pre-conceptive technology to determine a conceptus's gender without abortion or in-vitro fertilization. But until the sex selection argument unravels before technological innovation, women's rights to control their bodies must be defended against laws banning—or requiring—prenatal ultrasound and abortion.

6

Sex Selection Changes the Meaning of Procreation

President's Council on Bioethics

The President's Council on Bioethics advises the president of the United States on issues related to advancements in technology and biomedical science.

The practice of sex selection changes the meaning of reproduction. Reproduction should be about parents accepting their children for who they are, not because of their gender. Sex selection is also troubling because it leads to bias against women. Parents do not have the ethical right to control their children's sexual identity.

In considering the ethical implications of sex selection, we must attend especially to the social consequences not just of the *fact* of choice but of the *choices made*. For the private choices made by individuals, once aggregated, could produce major changes in a society's sex ratio, with profound implications for the entire community—and also its neighbors. Over the past several decades, disturbing evidence has accumulated of the widespread use of various medical technologies to choose the sex of one's child, with a strong preference for the male sex. The natural sex ratio at birth is 105 baby boys born for every 100 baby girls. But in several countries today the ratio approaches or even exceeds 120 baby boys born for every 100 girls. There is also evidence that the ratio at birth of boys

Presidential Council on Bioethics, *Choosing the Sex of Children, Beyond Therapy: Biotechnology and the Pursuit of Happiness*, Presidents Council on Bioethics, Washington, DC 2003.

to girls is rising among certain ethnic groups in the United States. This phenomenon especially calls out for our attention and demands a broad-ranging ethical and social evaluation. . . .

Sex Ratios Have Become Imbalanced

Even in just the short time that these various methods of sex selection have been available, they have had dramatic effects on sex ratios in many parts of the world. Generally, any variation in the sex ratio exceeding 106 boys born per 100 girls born can be assumed to be evidence of the practice of sex selection. Here, from most recent figures available, are just a few examples of skewed sex ratios around the world today. The sex ratio at birth of boys to 100 girls in Venezuela is 107.5; in Yugoslavia 108.6; in Egypt 108.7; in Hong Kong 109.7; in South Korea 110; in Pakistan 110.9; in Delhi, India, 117; in China 117; in Cuba 118; and in the Caucasus nations of Azerbaijan, Armenia, and Georgia, the sex ratio has reached as high as 120. (Although data is lacking regarding the techniques people in these countries use to produce these large shifts in the sex ratio, we suspect that sonography-plus-abortion is by far the most common.) While the sex ratio in the United States has remained stable at 104.8, certain American ethnic groups have seen a statistically significant rise in their sex ratios. In 1984 the sex ratio for Chinese-Americans was 104.6 and for Japanese Americans 102.6; in 2000, these ratios had risen respectively to 107.7 and 106.4.

Imbalances in the sex ratio are certainly not evenly spread across every region of the globe. However, one cannot but be impressed by the fact that distortions in the sex ratio afflict developed as well as underdeveloped nations. Hindu and Moslem populations as well as Christian populations, Western as well as non-Western nations, wealthy and educated regions as well as those that are less so. Although the practice is, for now, greater outside than within the United States, the other nations are mainly using technologies that we have developed (albeit for other purposes). One can only expect in the future that technologies of sex selection will be further refined and that new and cheaper technologies will emerge on the market. In the absence of some system of regulation, nothing stands in the way of a continuation and expansion of substantial distortions in the ratio, at least in some parts of the world and among some communities in the United States. . . .

Arguments on Both Sides

Although the practice of sex selection continues to grow, the American public debate over sex selection has never been aired in full. The new impetus to the growth of this practice, from multiculturalism to commercial interests, will make it difficult to slow its future spread. All the more reason to try now to evaluate its significance, beginning with the most common arguments for and against the practice.

There are a number of reasons given to support the practice of sex selection. The most common rationale today for sex selection is that it permits family balancing, enabling a couple to achieve its as-yet-unfulfilled wish to raise both sons and daughters. Many parents have had three or four girls (or boys) in a row, and really want a boy (or girl); effective sex selection would satisfy this wish without any risk of continued "failure." More generally, sex selection is defended on grounds that it could increase the happiness of the parents by enabling them to fulfill their desire for one or more sons or daughters. Sex selection is also supported because it may help to slow population growth (since many families continue to have children only to achieve a particular balance of boys and girls); because it may enable parents to fulfill religious or cultural expectations (since some cultures attach great importance to or impose special obligations on male heirs); and because it may make children feel more wanted and comfortable with their sex (since they will know that they were in fact chosen to be whichever sex they are).

In certain cultures, the desire of parents for sons is extremely powerful; in traditional Islam, for example, parents are expected to continue bearing children until they have at least one son. A strong preference for sons also appears prevalent in most (though not all) of the countries of Asia. Sex selection can therefore be defended on "multicultural grounds," as helping parents to achieve not merely individual preferences but also traditional and religious aims.

Sex selection has involved the abortion of female fetuses on a massive scale.

A common objection voiced against sex selection is that, in its most prevalent practice today, it almost always involves the abortion of (otherwise healthy) fetuses of the unwanted sex. However, sex selection by IVF [in vitro fertilization] with PGD [preimplantation genetic diagnosis] involves instead the selective transfer of embryos of the desired sex and the discarding of any embryos of the other sex: some people, for this reason, regard this approach as less morally objectionable than the one that requires abortion, while others see no moral difference. No such stigma attaches to the practice, still nascent, of sex selection by sperm sorting: whether used with artificial insemination or in conjunction with IVF, sperm sorting reduces the need to discard embryos of the unwanted sex. Should ongoing research eventually produce selective spermicides that would permit sex selection via natural intercourse, all such objections to the means would be much diminished or even disappear. We would be left to evaluate only the end itself.

The objection most often raised to sex selection, especially as it is practiced throughout the world today, is that it reflects and contributes to bias or discrimination against women. Sex selection has involved the abortion of female fetuses on a massive scale, or, in a few cases only, the selection of male embryos over female ones for implantation. As we have seen, sex ratios in some communities have been altered sharply in a very short period of time. Yet, criticism of this phenomenon has tended to be muted because of the connection between sex selection and abortion; those who support the right to an abortion have generally been reluctant to argue that abortion for the sake of sex selection should be restricted. The "pro-choice" idea of "every child a wanted child" establishes the rule in reproductive matters of the supremacy of parental "wants." Ironically, the "right to choose," which was and is defended in the name of equality for women, has in this way made permissible the disproportionate choice of aborting female fetuses. It is open to question whether the cause of equality has been well served by this development.

Paradoxically, the anti-female bias thought by critics to be implicit in sex selection might in fact redound to the advantage of women, at least regarding marriage: their relative scarcity could give them greater selectivity, choice, and control of partners. In certain Asian countries, for example, where the ratio of boys to girls at birth has been severely skewed by sex selection, young men of marriageable age are already facing a severe shortage of young women to marry. Thus one might oppose sex selection as much for the actual harm it does to men as for the prejudice it expresses against women.

But sex selection is ethically troubling for reasons that go beyond both its potentially discriminatory use and the necessity, under current procedures, of destroying fetuses or embryos of the unwanted sex. One of the fundamental issues has to do with the limits of liberty.

Not a Reproductive Liberty

As we noted earlier, few policy makers or opinion leaders argue openly in favor of sex selection. Rather, the assumption is made that our most cherished ideals of individual autonomy and the right to choose preclude an unambiguous condemnation of sex selection or public policies that might curtail it. Yet this assumption is questionable.

It is far from clear that either the moral or the legal right to procreate includes the right to choose the sex . . . of one's children.

Our society, to be sure, deeply cherishes liberty and rightfully gives a wide berth to its exercise. But liberty is never without its limits. In the case of actions that are purely self-regarding—that is, actions that affect only ourselves—society tends to give the greatest protections to personal freedom. But as we move outwards, away from purely self-regarding actions to those actions that affect others, our liberty is necessarily more liable to societal and governmental oversight and restraint. Sex selection clearly does not belong in the category of purely self-regarding action. The parents' actions (their choice of a boy or a girl) are directed not only toward themselves but also toward the child-to-be.

One might argue that, since each child must be either a girl or a boy, the parents' actions in selecting the sex do not constitute much of an intrusion on the prospective child's freedom and well being. But the binary choice among highly natural and familiar types hardly makes the choice a trivial one. And having one's sex foreordained by another is different from having it determined by the lottery of sexual union. There is thus at least a prima facie case for suggesting that the power to foreordain or control the nature of one's child's sexual identity is not encompassed in the protected sphere of inviolable reproductive liberty. It is far from clear that either the moral or the legal right to procreate includes the right to choose the sex—or other traits—of one's children.

But it is not only that sex selection affects the individual child-to-be that puts it in a class of actions fit for oversight, regulation, and (perhaps) curtailment. Sex selection, if practiced widely, can also have powerful societal effects that reach far beyond individuals and their families to the nation as a whole. The dramatic alteration in sex ratios in such countries as South Korea and Cuba bears this out. Whether or not one views the preference of individuals for sons over daughters as rational, taken together these individual preferences could and do have serious society-wide effects. . . .

In practicing sex selection our acceptance of our children becomes conditional.

In a previous Council report, on human cloning, we emphasized how cloning-to-produce-children alters the very nature and meaning of human procreation, implicitly turning it (at least in concept) into a form of manufacture and opening the door to a new eugenics. Sex selection raises related concerns.

Sex Selection Means Conditional Love

The salient fact about human procreation in its natural context is that children are not *made* but *begotten*. By this we mean that children are the issue of our love, not the product of our wills. A man and a woman do not produce or choose a *particular* child, as they might buy a particular brand of soap; rather, they stand in relation to their child as recipients of a gift. Gifts and blessings we learn to accept as gratefully as we can; products of our wills we try to shape in accordance with our wants and desires. Procreation as traditionally understood invites acceptance, not reshaping or engineering. It encourages us to see that we do not own our children and that our children exist not simply for our fulfillment. Of course, parents seek to shape and nurture their children in a variety of ways; but being a parent also means being open to the *unbidden* and *unelected* in life.

Sex selection challenges this fundamental understanding of procreation and parenthood. When we select for sex we are, consciously or not, seeking to design our children according to our wants and desires. The choice is never merely innocent or indifferent, since a host of powerful expectations goes into the selection of a boy or a girl. In choosing one sex over the other, we are necessarily making a statement about what we expect of that child—even if it is nothing more than that the child should provide sexual balance in the family. As fathers, we may want a son to go fishing with; or as mother, we may want a daughter to dress for the prom. The problem goes deeper than sexual stereotyping, however. For it could also be the case that we may want a daughter who will become president to show that women are the equal of men. But in making this kind of selection we have hardly escaped the problem, for the child's sexual identity would be determined by us in order to fulfill some particular desire of our own. If this were not the case then there would be no felt need to choose the sex of our child in the first place. And thus does it happen that in practicing sex selection our acceptance of our children becomes conditional—a stance that is fundamentally incompatible with the deeper meanings of procreation and parenthood.

7

Sex Selection Can Lead to Gender Discrimination

American College of Obstetricians and Gynecologists

The American College of Obstetricians and Gynecologists is America's leading organization of professionals who provide health care for women and seek to improve the quality of that care.

Sex selection technology should not be used to balance the gender ratio in families. When the technology is utilized in that manner, it can lead to sex discrimination and inequality between the sexes. While the use of sex selection to prevent serious sex-linked genetic disorders is ethical, health-care workers must foster open communication with their patients to ensure that they are not unintentionally participating in sex selection for nonmedical reasons.

The principal medical indication for sex selection is known or suspected risk of sex-linked genetic disorders. For example, 50% of males born to women who carry the gene for hemophilia will have this condition. By identifying the sex of the preimplantation embryo or fetus, a woman can learn whether or not the 50% risk of hemophilia applies, and she can receive appropriate prenatal counseling. To ensure that surviving offspring will not have this condition, some women at risk for transmitting hemophilia choose to abort male fetuses or choose not to transfer male embryos. Where the

American College of Obstetricians and Gynecologists, "Sex Selection," *ACOG Committee Opinion*, no. 360, February 2007. Copyright © 2007 American College of Obstetricians and Gynecologists. All rights reserved. Reproduced by permission.

marker or gene for a sex-linked genetic disorder is known, selection on the basis of direct identification of affected embryos or fetuses, rather than on the basis of sex, is possible. Direct identification has the advantage of avoiding the possibility of aborting an unaffected fetus or deciding not to transfer unaffected embryos. Despite the increased ability to identify genes and markers, in certain situations, sex determination is the only current method of identifying embryos or fetuses potentially affected with sex-linked disorders.

Inevitably, identification of sex occurs whenever karyotyping [a testing method using dye and fluorescent lights to determine the chromosomal characteristics of a cell] is performed. When medical indications for genetic karyotyping do not require information about sex chromosomes, the prospective parent(s) may elect not to be told the sex of the fetus.

Other reasons sex selection is requested are personal, social, or cultural in nature. For example, the prospective parent(s) may prefer that an only or first-born child be of a certain sex or may desire a balance of sexes in the completed family. . . .

Reasons for Sex Selection

Health care providers may participate unknowingly in sex selection when information about the sex of a fetus results from a medical procedure performed for some other purpose. For example, when a procedure is done to rule out medical disorders in the fetus, the sex of a fetus may become known and may be used for sex selection without the health care provider's knowledge.

The American College of Obstetricians and Gynecologists' Committee on Ethics maintains that when a medical procedure is done for a purpose other than obtaining information about the sex of a fetus but will reveal the fetus's sex, this information should not be withheld from the pregnant woman who requests it. This is because this information legally and ethically belongs to the patient. As a consequence, it might be difficult for health care providers to avoid the possibility of unwittingly participating in sex selection. To minimize the possibility that they will unknowingly participate in sex selection, physicians should foster open communication with patients aimed at clarifying patients' goals. Although health care providers may not ethically withhold medical information from patients who request it, they are not obligated to perform an abortion, or other medical procedure, to select fetal sex.

Four Ethical Positions

With regard to medical procedures performed for the express purpose of selecting the sex of a fetus, the following four potential ethical positions are outlined to facilitate discussion:

Position 1: Never participate in sex selection. Health care providers may never choose to perform medical procedures with the intended purpose of sex selection.

Position 2: Participate in sex selection when medically indicated. Health care providers may choose to perform medical procedures with the intended purpose of preventing sex-linked genetic disorders.

Position 3: Participate in sex selection for medical indications and for the purpose of family balancing. Health care providers may choose to perform medical procedures for sex selection when the patient has at least one child and desires a child of the other sex.

Position 4: Participate in sex selection whenever requested. Health care providers may choose to perform medical procedures for the purpose of sex selection whenever the patient requests such procedures.

The committee shares the concern expressed by the United Nations and the International Federation of Gynecology and Obstetrics that sex selection can be motivated by and reinforce the devaluation of women. The committee supports the ethical principle of equality between the sexes.

It often is impossible to ascertain patients' true motives for requesting sex selection procedures.

The committee rejects, as too restrictive, the position that sex selection techniques are always unethical (position 1). The committee supports, as ethically permissible, the practice of sex selection to prevent serious sex-linked genetic disorders (position 2). However, the increasing availability of testing for specific gene mutations is likely to make selection based on sex alone unnecessary in many of these cases. For example, it supports offering patients using assisted reproductive techniques the option of preimplantation genetic diagnosis for identification of male sex chromosomes if patients are at risk for transmitting Duchenne's muscular dystrophy. This position is consistent with the stance of equality between the sexes because it does not imply that the sex of a child itself makes that child more or less valuable.

Family Balancing Goes Against Gender Equality

Some argue that sex selection techniques can be ethically justified when used to achieve a "balance" in a family in which all current children are the same sex and a child of the opposite sex is desired (position 3). To achieve this goal, couples may request 1) sperm sorting by flow cytometry [a technique of sorting and identifying cells and their components] to enhance the probability of achieving a pregnancy of a particular sex, although these techniques are considered experimental; 2) transferring only embryos of one sex in assisted reproduction after embryo biopsy and preimplantation genetic diagnosis; 3) reducing, on the basis of sex, the number of fetuses in a multifetal pregnancy; or 4) aborting fetuses that are not of the desired sex. In these situations, individual parents may consistently judge sex selection to be an important personal or family goal and, at the same time, reject the idea that children of one sex are inherently more valuable than children of another sex.

Use of sex selection techniques for family balancing violates the norm of equality between the sexes.

Although this stance is, in principle, consistent with the principle of equality between the sexes, it nonetheless raises ethical concerns. First, it often is impossible to ascertain patients' true motives for requesting sex selection procedures. For example, patients who want to abort female fetuses because they value male offspring more than female offspring would be unlikely to espouse such beliefs openly if they thought this would lead physicians to deny their requests. Second, even when sex selection is requested for nonsexist reasons, the very idea of preferring a child of a particular sex may be interpreted as condoning sexist values and, hence, create a climate in which sex discrimination can more easily flourish. Even preconception techniques of sex selection may encourage such a climate. The use of flow cytometry is experimental, and preliminary reports indicate that achievement of a female fetus is not guaranteed. Misconception about the accuracy of this evolving technology coupled with a strong preference for a child of a particular sex may lead couples to terminate a pregnancy of the "undesired" sex.

The committee concludes that use of sex selection techniques for family balancing violates the norm of equality between the sexes; moreover, this ethical objection arises regardless of the timing of selection (i.e., preconception or postconception) or the stage of development of the embryo or fetus.

8

Sex Selection Will Not Lead to Gender Discrimination

Ronald Bailey

Ronald Bailey is the science correspondent for Reason *magazine and its Web site,* Reason Online.

The practice of sex selection will not lead to violence or a gender imbalance in Western nations. American parents who use sperm-sorting technology are largely seeking girls or want to balance the gender among their children. In addition, German and British parents have no preference about the sex of their children. These attitudes show that concerns over sex selection leading to a society of violent young men are groundless.

"Sex selection will cause a severe imbalance of the sexes," predicted left-wing sociologist Amitai Etzioni way back in 1968. Etzioni further prophesied that the practice would "soon" condemn millions of men to rape, prostitution, homosexuality, or enforced celibacy.

More recently, Brigham Young University [in Utah] political scientist Valerie M. Hudson and University of Kent [in Canterbury, England] research fellow Andrea M. den Boer argued in their book *Bare Branches: The Security Implications of Asia's Surplus Male Population* that growing sex ratio imbalances resulting from sex selection in China will create a hoodlum army of 30 million single men that by 2020 will be a menace to world peace.

Sex selection in India and China is achieved chiefly through ultrasound scans followed by the selective abortion of female fetuses. The natural sex ratio is about 105 boys per 100 girls, but in India it is now 113 boys per 100 girls and as high as 156 boys per 100 girls in some regions.

New Technologies Are Emerging

In China the sex ratio now is just shy of 120 boys per 100 girls. Both China and India now ban the use of abortion for sex selection. Should those of us living in the developed world worry about skewed sex ratios in our own countries? After all, all sorts of nifty new biomedical technologies besides selective abortions are becoming available to make sex selection ever more feasible.

For example, the Genetics and IVF [in vitro fertilization] (GIVF) Institute in Fairfax, Virginia, is pioneering preconception sex selection by means of a system that segregates sperm that will produce girls from those that will produce boys. Joseph Schulman, the founder of GIVF, explained how his clinic's MicroSort sperm-segregation system works at the First International Conference on Ethics, Science and Moral Philosophy of Assisted Human Reproduction at the Royal Society in London [in September 2004].

Of the more than 3,000 sperm-sorting cycles requested by patients, 77 percent have been seeking to produce girls.

MicroSort technology tags sperm bearing X chromosomes (those which determine females) and sperm bearing Y chromosomes (those which determine males) with a fluorescent dye so that they can be segregated into different batches. The dye harmlessly attaches to the DNA molecules that make up genes. Female-determining X chromosomes are much bigger than male-determining Y chromosomes, which means that human sperm carrying X chromosomes have 2.8 percent more DNA than do sperm with Y chromosomes.

Thus, X-sperm soak up more of the fluorescent dye and glow more brightly. This difference in brightness allows flow cytometry machines to detect and separate the X- from the Y-bearing sperm. The sperm-separating technique is not perfect: According to the latest data, batches of sperm intended to produce males typically contain 75 percent Y chromosome sperm. The female batches contain 91 percent X chromosome sperm.

Once the sperm have been segregated, they may be used in either artificial insemination or in vitro fertilization to produce a child of the desired sex. Using sex-segregated sperm in artificial insemination sidesteps the contentious debate over the moral status of embryos, since fertilization takes place straight in the would-be mothers' wombs. The cost per cycle of MicroSort's service is about $3,000.

Not a Threat to Gender Ratios

For those worried about whether such sex selection technology will radically skew U.S. sex ratios, Schulman's clinical data should be soothing. Of the more than 3,000 sperm-sorting cycles requested by patients, 77 percent have been seeking to produce girls. Most parents want to use MicroSort to achieve "family balancing," that is, to have a child of the opposite sex to the first one, or to balance out families that now have all girls or all boys.

Another reason to use sperm segregation is to avoid the 500 or so inheritable X-linked diseases, such as hemophilia, that afflict boys. Boys are more vulnerable to these diseases because they inherit only a single X chromosome from their mothers, whereas girls inherit two, one from each parent. If there is a faulty gene on one X chromosome, the undamaged one on the other X chromosome shields girls from its deleterious effects. But boys, who have only one X chromosome paired with a much smaller Y chromosome, will suffer from the disease if they inherit the X chromosome with the faulty gene.

Allowing parents in the West access to sex selection won't result in bands of violent horny young men whose only access to sex is rape, prostitution, or homosexuality.

More evidence that the West was unlikely to go the way of China and India was presented at the Royal Society conference by German bioethicist Edgar Dahl from the University of Giessen. He cited updated surveys from Germany, the United Kingdom, and the United States that found no strong gender preferences.

In Germany, 76 percent of respondents didn't care about the sex of their first child, while 14 percent would prefer a boy and 10 percent would prefer a girl. When asked if they might consider using MicroSort, 94 percent of Germans rejected it out of hand. When asked if they might consider using cost-free magic pills, a pink one for girls and a blue one for boys, to select their children's sex, 92 said no, they'd turn down those pills.

Seventy-three percent of Britons had no preference about the sex of their first-born child. Sixty-eight percent of Britons would like to have equal numbers of girls and boys in their families, compared to only 30 percent of Germans. A majority of Americans did express a preference about the sex of their first-born: 39 percent would prefer a boy and 19 percent would prefer a girl. Forty-nine percent of Americans wanted an equal number of boys and girls in their families, and 18 percent could imagine taking advantage of MicroSort-type sex selection service.

Dahl argued that the only valid justification for limiting parents' liberty to select their children's sex might be a clear and present threat that a society's sex ratio is about to become radically unbalanced. "In the West, there is no evidence at all that there is a threat to the sex ratio," Dahl concluded. So Etzioni's dire predictions have proven to be wrong; allowing parents in the West access to sex selection won't result in bands of violent horny young men whose only access to sex is rape, prostitution, or homosexuality.

During the question-and-answer period at the Royal Society conference, a physician from India claimed that if MicroSort became widely available in his country, 90 percent of parents would choose to have only boys. Thus, he argued, sex selection should be banned there. However, the physician noted that skewed sex ratios seem to be a problem chiefly in the Hindu community. Indian Muslim and Christian sex ratios were close to the natural rate. He also noted that in families in which the women were literate, the sex ratios are also close to the natural rate. "That seems to me to make a strong case, not for banning sex selection, but for more and better education of women," replied Dahl. Seems about right to me too.

9

Sex Selection Leads to Abortions in Asia

Carla Power

Carla Power is a writer based in London.

Gender imbalance is a serious problem in Asia, particularly China and India. Boys greatly outnumber girls in these societies due to the practice of female feticide and infanticide. Population control programs that encourage people to have small families have worsened the problem because Asian traditions consider girls to be economic liabilities; therefore, women only want to give birth to sons, who can help provide for their families. Violence against women is another consequence of gender imbalance and will remain a problem if governments cannot successfully enforce laws that prevent sex-selective abortions.

Grey hair pulled into a tidy bun, blood-orange sari crisp, Sangam Satyavathi marches into the hospital, her team scurrying after her. She is on a raid. As district health officer for Hyderabad [India], Dr Satyavathi is on a "sting operation"—a surprise visit to a maternity hospital to check its ultrasound records. A nervous knot of doctors and nurses forms around her, under a portrait of the baby Krishna and an advertisement for a General Electric ultrasound machine. This features a pregnant belly and the slogan "We bring good things to life". Satyavathi and her team frown over ledgers and a pile of Form Fs, required whenever a pregnant woman has an ultrasound scan. Like all the other hospitals in Hyderabad District, this one has been ordered, as part of a local campaign against female foeticide, to present detailed records of any such procedures.

"No reports," says Satyavathi, frowning. "And no consent forms."

"Consent form we are not taking, madam," ventures a doctor.

More poring over ledgers. "You haven't submitted your forms on time."

"Next time, madam."

"Next time?" she asks. "Now we are going to seize the machine."

Dr Satyavathi's men go to work. They shroud the ultrasound machine in a sheet, then wrap it in lashings of surgical gauze. They drip red molten wax on the knots. Satyavathi whips out a five-rupee coin and presses it to the wax, sealing the suspect machine with the design of the three-headed lion, symbol of the Indian government.

"You see," she says grimly. "The act is so powerful."

Preventing Sex-Selective Abortion

The Prenatal Diagnostic Techniques Act [PNDT Act] is powerful indeed, but rarely enforced. Passed after India realised that modern medical techniques such as ultrasound scans and amniocenteses were frequently being used to identify female foetuses—which are then aborted—the PNDT Act requires the registration of all ultrasound machines, and bans doctors from revealing the sex of the foetus to expectant parents. The 1994 law was an attempt to reverse India's rampant use of sex-selective abortion, and the lopsided sex ratio this has produced. India's 2001 census showed that there were 927 girls to every 1,000 boys, down from 945:1,000 in 1991 and 962:1,000 in 1981. Until recently, no doctors had been put in prison under the PNDT Act. But [in March 2006] a doctor was jailed for three years after telling an undercover investigator that her foetus was female, and hinting that she could abort it. Arvind

Kumar, Hyderabad district collector and Satyavathi's boss, sees the law as the only practical tool for tackling India's female foeticide epidemic. Doctors who practise sex-selective abortion, he says, "like any other criminals, should be treated like criminals".

It is uncertain how many such crimes have been committed. A January study in the *Lancet* [British medical journal] estimated that ten million female foeticides had occurred in India over the past two decades. Both the Indian Medical Association and anti-sex-selection activists disputed the findings, saying the numbers were too high. While the numbers may be a matter of debate, the general trend is not: the ratio of girls to boys in India has been dwindling over the past two decades. In 1991, not a single district in India had a child sex ratio of less than 800:1,000. By 2001, there were 14.

"What we're dealing with," says Sabu George, India's leading activist, "is a genocide."

The prospects are even bleaker elsewhere in Asia. In South Korea and China, official numbers suggest that there are 855 girls for every 1,000 boys. In the case of China, independent experts put it even lower, at 826:1,000. Whichever is correct, the Chinese demographic picture is more unbalanced than back in 1990, when the statistics showed 901 girls for every 1,000 boys. Today, in parts of Hainan and Guangdong Provinces, the ratio is 769:1,000. The Chinese scenario has already produced a glut of bachelors, which experts say will only get worse. A 2002 article in *International Security* magazine estimated that by 2020 there will be up to 33 million *guang guan* ("bare branches"), as these young, unmarried men are known. Some demographers have put the figure even higher, at 40 million.

History of Infanticide

The unwanted girl has a long history in Asia. The first written record of female infanticide dates back to Japan's Tokugawa period, between 1600 and 1868, when there were nine times as many boys born as girls. A British colonial official in India recorded cases of female infanticide as long ago as the 1780s. In rural India today, there are *dais*, traditional birth attendants, who still know how to get rid of unwanted baby girls. Classic methods include feeding the newborn rice or salt, or smothering the baby with a pillow.

In recent decades, female infanticide has been eclipsed by modern methods of sex determination, including amniocentesis or ultrasound scan, followed by abortion. Activists say female foeticide is merely the first assault on Indian women, and cannot be seen as separate from the whole life cycle of anti-girl practices in India: girl-child neglect, early marriage, the dowry system, domestic violence and honour killings. "Being a girl," says Sabu George, "is considered a congenital defect."

Asia's dearth of girls, say researchers, is partly a function of official reproductive health policies.

It is tempting to dismiss Asia's female foeticide problem as a product of the sexism of "backward" societies. To be sure, the problem stems from traditional belief systems favouring boys, but the prevalence of sex selection is an unexpected side effect of modernity. Female foeticide has been boosted by precisely the trends that make China and India the great success stories of the Noughties [the decade encompassing the years 2000 to 2009]: economic liberalisation, growing affluence, increased access to technology, and controlled population explosions.

Asia's dearth of girls, say researchers, is partly a function of official reproductive health policies. In the late 20th century, both China and India embarked on population-control programmes. In China, from the 1950s to the 1970s, when the government needed female workers, female infanticide dropped to the lowest levels the country had ever known, a

2004 study in the *Journal of Population Research* reported. After 1979, however, when the infamous one-child policy was introduced, female infanticide and foeticide became more common. In India, the muscular public health campaigns of the 1970s and 1980s drummed home the official line: happy families were small ones. Abortion, legalised in 1970, "was pursued with an almost patriotic zeal," recalls Dr Puneet Bedi, a Delhi obstetrician and anti-sex-selection activist. Tellingly, the Indian states that did particularly well in curbing population growth—the Punjab, Delhi and Haryana among them—are today those with the most skewed sex ratios. "A large part of the small family ideal is achieved by eliminating girls," says George. Pressurised by the government to keep their families small, and by society to produce boys, Indian women turned to modern technology to ensure that they got their treasured sons.

India's new open markets have made it easier. Economic liberalisation in the early 1990s brought not just foreign cars and the outsourcing boom, but the rise of what Bedi calls "medical entrepreneurship". Easy credit and aggressive marketing by foreign companies made it possible for thousands of clinics to buy ultrasound machines. "The ultrasound machine was marketed like Coca-Cola," Bedi says. Between 1988 and 2003, there was a 33-fold increase in the annual manufacture of ultrasound equipment in India. Doctors advertised their possibilities widely. "Boy or girl?" asked adverts, before the PNDT Act outlawed them. A 2005 report by the Geneva Centre for the Democratic Control of Armed Forces noted that sex selection had become "a booming business" not only in India, but also in China and South Korea.

Girls Are Expendable

In India, the recent *Lancet* study found sex-selective abortion was far more prevalent among the urban middle classes than the illiterate poor: the more educated the mother, the less likely she was to give birth to a second child who was a girl. Though the practice has recently begun to spread to remote areas and to the south, it has been most widely practised in cities, particularly in the north. It is rare among Dalits and remote tribes and common among Sikhs and Jains, historically wealthy business communities. In Delhi, the leafiest suburbs have the worst sex ratios. Shailaja Chandra, a top-tier civil servant, says that preference for boys is common among the capital's elites.

"They want to keep property in the family," she says. "Because boys traditionally inherit the wealth, people want boys."

For many activists, India's female foeticide problem is entwined with the consumer society the country has become over the past 15 years. If one can order a BMW, goes the mindset, one can order a boy. Mira Shiva, a member of both the National Commission for Women and the National Commission on Population, sees the issue of female foeticide as just one example of the rise in violent crime against women, created by India's quicksilver modernisation. "We're going through a time of increasing consumerism and materialism, where our values are changing," she says. "Market-wise, things that are deemed not of value are expendable."

Boy-preference is so ingrained in the Indian family system that many women don't feel they have done their wifely duty until they produce a son.

Other traditions have helped make girls seem expendable in Asia. Usually boys, not girls, carry on the family name. In Hinduism, it is the son who lights the funeral pyre when his parents die. In China and South Korea, ancestor-worship rituals are performed by sons and grandsons. In both China and India, boys are viewed as pension schemes, supporting their parents in old age.

If boys are a boon, girls are a liability. In India, the birth of a girl eventually entails a dowry, an increasingly expensive proposition. Where the grandmothers of today recall going to their husbands' homes with a pot or two and a few rupees, a modern dowry can cost hundreds of thousands of rupees. Girls are viewed as both an economic drain and a hassle. The protection of their virginity—central to family honour—creates further stress for parents. Boy-preference is so ingrained in the Indian family system that many women don't feel they have done their wifely duty until they produce a son. "They want to bend their heads, like sheep being slaughtered," observes Dr Soubhagya Bhat, an obstetrician-gynaecologist in Belgaum, Karnataka. "The only way they feel their life is fulfilled is if they produce a son."

Violence Against Women Is Rising

Governments are trying to change the conventional mindset. In 2003, India's national government launched a policy of paying homeless women money to help with their newborn babies: girls get double the rupees boys do. In Delhi, the Directorate of Family Welfare has recently come out with a clutch of "Respect the Girls" advertisements, with slogans such as: "If you kill daughters, you will keep searching for mothers, daughters and wives" and "Indira Gandhi and Mother Teresa: your daughter can be one of them!" They haven't worked. The latest statistics suggest that Delhi's sex ratio stands at roughly 814 girls to 1,000 boys. This is down from 845:1,000 in 2003.

If such trends continue, the future could be nightmarish. In their 2004 book *Bare Branches: The Security Implications of Asia's Surplus Male Population*, the political scientists Andrea den Boer and Valerie Hudson argue that the existence of all these millions of frustrated Asian bachelors will boost crime and lawlessness. They speculate that, to find an outlet for the continent's sex-starved males, Asian governments might even need to resort to fomenting wars. Indian activists also fear that the girl shortage will create a hyper-macho society.

Spiralling numbers of rapes and rates of violence will lead to the increasing sequestration of women. Men with money will be able to afford wives, who will quickly become a status symbol. "Powerful men would maintain *zanankhanas* [harems] to demonstrate their power and influence," writes the activist R P Ravindra. Poorer men, "finding no companions, might resort to any means to force a woman into a sexual/marital relationship."

In pockets of India, this has already begun. In Haryana and the Punjab, home to India's most unbalanced sex ratios, trafficking in women has skyrocketed. Men from these wealthy areas are purchasing wives from impoverished eastern states such as East Bengal and Bihar. This trend of "killing girls in the womb in western states is hurting girls in eastern states who have survived in the womb", argues Kamal Kumar Pandey, a lawyer with the Shakti Vahini network, an anti-trafficking NGO [nongovernmental organization].

Rishi Kant, the network's founder, brandishes a recent snap-shot showing a bloody, decapitated corpse: a 12-year-old bride wearing a yellow dress. The girl was murdered by the man who bought her for 25,000 rupees, says Kant, because she had refused to sleep with his brother. Tales of violence against bought women, and of brothers sharing wives, are increasingly common in parts of northern India.

The spectre of millions of lawless bachelors seems a far cry from the bureaucratic world-view of Arvind Kumar in Hyderabad. If India's officials could just implement the PNDT Act, he believes, the demographic tide could be reversed. He is just 18 months into the campaign, and so he sounds cautious, but the latest figures suggest that Hyderabad's sex ratio might be tilting back into balance. He tells of a letter he received recently from a 13-year-old girl who was being belittled by her family for not being a son. Just hearing of his work, she had written, had given her strength enough not to be ashamed of being a girl.

10

Policies Against Gender-Related Abortions in China Have Not Been Effective

Nie Jing-Bao

Nie Jing-Bao is a Bioethics Centre senior lecturer at the Dunedin School of Medicine at the University of Otago in New Zealand.

Efforts by the Chinese government to prevent gender imbalance have been ineffective. Prenatal diagnosis for sex and sex-selective abortions have been banned in China, but the number of boys born continues to be significantly higher than the number of girls. This imbalance may be occurring because of female infanticide and the abandonment of female babies, practices that have been used in China throughout its history.

The duty of citizens to follow state birth control policies has long been mandated in Chinese law. In 1980, the Fifth National People's Congress passed a revised marriage law that obligated both partners to practice family planning. In 1982, the same body passed a new constitution that set out the government's aims very clearly: "The state's family planning program is designed to ensure that population increase keeps pace with its plans for economic and social development"; and on the family level, "Both the husband and the wife have an obligation to practice family planning."

China Is Not Pro-Abortion

On the role of abortion in population control policy, the government insists that abortion is not preferred as a method of family planning and birth control. It has repeatedly emphasized that abortion is a "remedial measure" or "back-up method" (*bujiu cuoshi*). In the words of the Chinese government's White Paper on human rights in China, the family planning policy,

> has consistently given first place to contraception and the protection of women's and children's health. . . . The government strongly opposes any form of coerced abortion. Abortion is only a remedial measure when contraception fails, and is performed under voluntary and safe and secure conditions.

The White Paper on family planning points out that as the birth rate in China has fallen sharply, the ratio of abortions to live births remains at approximately 0.3:1—making China's abortion rate about average compared with other countries.

Contrary to the impression of many Westerners, not all abortions are legal in China. Termination for the purpose of sex selection, which has been made easier through modern methods of prenatal sex diagnosis, is clearly prohibited by various regulations. For many reasons, including the traditional value placed on male offspring to continue the bloodline and the need for security for elderly people, especially in countryside, many Chinese still prefer to have at least one male child. Over the centuries, Chinese doctors have pursued many methods of predicting the sex of the fetus, including taking the pulse of the pregnant woman. According to traditional Chinese medicine, male and female fetuses produce different pulse patterns in mothers. While the accuracy of such traditional methods is doubtful, advances in modern biomedical technology, such as B ultrasonic, have made relatively accurate prenatal sex diagnosis both possible and financially feasible.

Regulations Against Prenatal Diagnosis

Prenatal diagnosis of sex and selective abortion for males has been outlawed in a series of regulations. As early as September 1986, the National Commission for Family Planning and the Ministry of Health circulated a regulation promulgated by the authorities in Beijing that prohibited prenatal diagnosis at the request of the mother, except when used by authorized hospitals to diagnose certain hereditary diseases. Individuals or clinics violating this ban were liable for penalties. In May 1989, September 1990, and April 1993, the 1986 decree was reaffirmed in the circulars issued by the two national authorities. Sex identification of the fetus using medical techniques (except when necessary on medical grounds) and selective abortion for nonmedical reasons are strictly prohibited in the Law on Maternal and Infant Health Care (1994), the Law on Population and Family Planning (2001), and the comprehensive regulation on this subject issued jointly by the National Committee for Family Planning, the Ministry of Health, and the National Administrative and Supervisory Bureau of Drugs in 2002.

Taken together, these regulations offer three grounds for prohibition. First, prenatal diagnosis presents a threat to the family planning program, as some pregnant women, motivated by preference for a boy, would continue with an unauthorized pregnancy if they knew the fetus was male. Second, prenatal screening would lead many to abort female fetuses, creating an unbalanced sex ratio that would eventually produce serious social problems and endanger the long-term stability of the nation. Third, the use of such medical techniques is said to constitute a serious breach of medical ethics on the part of the physician involved—although the precise nature of the breach is not specified.

Gender Disparity and Infanticide

However, the current extraordinarily high ratio of male to female newborns in China shows that these regulations have proved much less effective than policy makers intended. According to censuses taken in 1983 and 1990, in the 1980s the ratio of male to female newborns varied between 108.5 (1981) and 113.8 (1989). The ratio has since spiraled to 117 in 2000, resulting in much concern and discussion. In a semiofficial article, demographer Tu Ping attributes the increasing incidence of male births to two factors: failure to report female births and selective abortion. For Tu, "The abnormality of sex ratios among newborns and infants in our country has profound social, economic, cultural, and historical causes. . . . We cannot attribute this problem simply to the implementation of the family planning program." The author deplores the statistical distortion resulting from the underreporting of female newborns. He further argues that selective abortion and the high mortality of female infants constitute an even graver problem because it disrupts the gender balance. Despite drawing attention to the abnormally high mortality rate among female children under five, and especially under one, the author never mentions infanticide as a possible cause.

It is inconceivable to deny any connection between female infanticide and family planning policies.

In addition to the use of contraception and abortion, many societies have resorted to infanticide and child abandonment as methods of limiting family size. The killing and abandonment of infants, especially females, has been practiced from very early times in China. For centuries, infanticide was not deemed a straightforward illegal act, partly because the social, moral, and legal control exercised by parents over their children extended to the power of life and death. Although clearly illegal in contemporary China, infanticide and abandonment still occur. Just as the demand for selective abortion is often attributed to the traditional valuing of males over females, infanticide is officially defined as a "feudalistic evil." The White Paper on human rights in China expressed the official position:

> Infanticide through drowning and abandoning female babies is an evil custom left over from feudal times. Although the practice has been greatly reduced, it still lingers on in a few remote places. Chinese laws explicitly forbid the drowning of infants and other actions that would harm them. China has adopted practical and effective measures to wipe out infanticide as well as to investigate and prosecute offenders.

Chinese law does in fact proscribe killing, abandoning, or abusing infants. The Marriage Law of 1980 prohibits "the drowning of infants and other actions that would lead to injury or death." The 1982 Constitution extends the protection of the state to the family, including the mother and child, and prohibits abuse of the elderly, women, and children. In the official discourse, therefore, just as the abnormally high ratio of male to female newborns bears no relation to the birth control program, it is the "pernicious influence of feudalism" that is responsible for the killing and abandonment of female infants. Given the existence of the practice for centuries in China, it is certainly wrong to say that all contemporary cases of infanticide are a direct result of the birth control program. Nevertheless, it is inconceivable to deny any connection between female infanticide and family planning policies. Of course, the continuation of female infanticide as well as the severely unbalanced birth ratio were never intended by policy makers. But any social policy has the potential to yield unintended negative consequences as well as intended benefits.

11

The United Nations Ignores Gender-Related Abortions in China and India

Douglas A. Sylva

Douglas A. Sylva is a senior fellow at the Catholic Family and Human Rights Institute, a research and education institute that focuses on international social policy.

Millions of babies are aborted or killed shortly after birth because they are girls, particularly in India and China. Efforts by the [George W.] Bush administration to stop this tragedy have been thwarted by the European Union and feminists, who believe that abortion should be allowed for any reason, even if it means girls are aborted disproportionately. For example, sex-selective abortion has become particularly common among wealthy Chinese women.

It is a wonderful case of man-bites-dog, but don't expect to see this headline in any newspaper: "[George W.] Bush administration's efforts to protect women through United Nations action thwarted by European Union."

Yet that is exactly what happened at the [2007] Commission on the Status of Women [CSW], where the United States' intention to help women (in this case, girls) ran afoul of dominant feminist orthodoxy. The Bush administration introduced a resolution condemning the killing of girls, because they are girls. Such acts include old-fashioned infanticide, the kind of cultural practice the British tried to stamp out in the bygone days of colonial India, as well as the ever more popular use of modern sonogram technology in order to identify and eliminate girls before they are born—what is called sex-selective abortion.

And this is where the United States met the opposition of the European Union and its allies: abortion-on-demand orthodoxy seems to mean women's total freedom to choose, even if that choice eliminates the next generation of women, for the very reason that they are women.

The Crisis of "Missing" Girls

The Bush administration's concern about infanticide and sex-selective abortion is not exaggerated; although numbers are difficult to establish, most demographers believe that millions of girls are now killed in this manner every year. The British medical journal *Lancet* recently surmised that there were perhaps 100 million "missing" girls in the world, girls not allowed to grow into women. China is the largest offender; in many regions, some as large and as highly populated as average-sized countries, there are now 130 boys born for every 100 girls (the normal ratio is 104 boys to 100 girls). Beyond the individual injustices involved, this creates a potential demographic calamity. Nobody knows what will happen to a society in which 40 million men cannot find wives, but, already, there are reports of widespread rapes, forced marriages, and human trafficking. In ten years' time, when the problem is more acute, the Chinese government might even find it necessary to send its excess men on a military "adventure" of some kind, in order to mitigate the social instability at home.

India is the second largest offender, proving that the problem transcends any particular culture. In fact the practice of sex-selective abortion is spreading throughout nearly every region on earth. There are four cultural factors that must be present for sex-selective abortion to arise: a traditional preference for sons, reduced fertility and family size, availability of sonogram technology, and cultural acceptance of abortion. It is these four factors, and the resulting sex-imbalance now so apparent in countless maternity wards, playgrounds and classrooms, that link such disparate nations as Libya and Luxembourg, Egypt and El Salvador.

Sex-selective abortion is especially prevalent among rich, urban, educated women in China.

It is perhaps obvious why sex-selective abortion is an embarrassment to feminism: while the preference for sons is deeply rooted in history, the other factors, such as reduced family size and cultural acceptance of abortion, are central pillars of feminist thought. Since at least the 1995 Beijing Women's Conference, feminist champions have argued that international "gender justice" could only be established if women possessed the reproductive rights necessary to reduce their family sizes, thereby liberating them for higher education and successful careers. This is as close to established wisdom as is found at the United Nations, and it is so dominant that there is even a phrase—the "gender perspective"—suggesting that all problems, from peace keeping, to land mine removal, to water supply management, could be solved if they were examined through this proper feminist point-of-view.

A Feminist Problem

So imagine the shock and shame when it became obvious that many of these newly-liberated women have been using their liberty to abort their own unborn girls. Research has even suggested that sex-selective abortion is especially prevalent among rich, urban, educated women in China, the pioneers, the type of women presumably leading the world into a genderless future. It is never pleasant to be forced to admit that one's revolutionaries have begun to devour their own.

And then there is abortion, itself. The European Union's civil society allies at the United Nations openly campaign for an international right to abortion-on-demand—and abortion-on-demand must really mean abortion-for-any-reason. So when China considered prohibiting sex-selective abortion in 2002, the Center for Reproductive Rights (CRR), perhaps the most influential pro-abortion nongovernmental organization, labeled the proposal "problematic." Sex-selective abortion remains legal in China to this day.

CRR was certainly on the scene during the recent negotiations, advising the European Union, China, and India to reject the U.S. resolution in condemning the practice. When the United States refused to let the subject drop and demanded that it at least be mentioned in a lesser document, the word abortion was not used and the problem was blamed simply on good old-fashioned male chauvinism—son preference. At the end of the session, in the final U.S. "Explanation of Position," the United States pointedly observed that, "We are happy that the document condemns female infanticide and 'harmful practices of prenatal sex selection,' which is universally understood to include sex-selective abortion, even if some delegations insisted that this practice not be called by its real name."

As strange as it may sound, under President George W. Bush the United States has perhaps the finest feminist record of any nation at the United Nations—if feminism exists to address grave and profound injustices against women. It has been the United States, for instance, which has raised such issues as trafficking in women, sexual exploitation, and sex tourism. It was the United States that attempted to draw the world's attention to mass rapes being conducted in Burma (only to be told that the United Nations would not publicize the U.S. effort because America did not use the current dictator's name for his country, Myanmar). And now the United States is attempting to address sex-selective abortion.

The U.S. Explanation of Position concluded by stating that the outcome of the two weeks of negotiations "lends itself to the impression that the CSW is in danger of becoming a highly politicized body more concerned with preserving its ideological orthodoxy than in solving real problems facing real women and girls today." Seven years into the Bush administration, perhaps the biggest surprise is that the administration itself remains surprised when its good intentions are once again undermined by such ideological orthodoxy.

12

Sex Selection in China and India Could Lead to War

David Glenn

David Glenn is a senior reporter for the Chronicle of Higher Education.

Although there is debate over the validity of the conclusions, research suggests that the gender imbalance in China and India that has been the result of sex selection will lead to a generation of young men who are unable to find wives and who will turn to violence because they cannot form families. Wars and the formation of militant organizations may be a consequence of this rise in violence and disorder. Such conclusions have their basis in history, which has repeatedly shown the impact young single men have on society.

In a . . . [2004] book, *Bare Branches: Security Implications of Asia's Surplus Male Population* (MIT Press), Valerie M. Hudson and Andrea M. den Boer warn that the spread of sex selection is giving rise to a generation of restless young men who will not find mates. History, biology, and sociology all suggest that these "surplus males" will generate high levels of crime and social disorder, the authors say. Even worse, they continue, is the possibility that the governments of India and China will build up huge armies in order to provide a safety valve for the young men's aggressive energies.

"In 2020 it may seem to China that it would be worth it to have a very bloody battle in which a lot of their young men could die in some glorious cause," says Ms. Hudson, a professor of political science at Brigham Young University.

Those apocalyptic forecasts garnered a great deal of attention when the scholars first presented them, in the journal *International Security*, in 2002. "The thing that excites me about this research is how fundamental demography is," says David T. Courtwright, a professor of history at the University of North Florida and author of *Violent Land: Single Men and Social Disorder from the Frontier to the Inner City* (Harvard University Press, 1996), a study of sex ratios and murder rates in American history. "The basic idea that they have, that in some sense demography is social destiny—that's a very powerful idea."

But other experts are unpersuaded. They say that Ms. Hudson and Ms. den Boer's argument rests too heavily on a few isolated historical cases, and that the authors have failed to establish a systematic correlation between sex ratios and violence. Critics also suggest that the argument promotes false stereotypes of men and masculinity, and that the authors do not offer detailed knowledge of Asian societies and political systems. Offspring sex selection is indeed a serious problem, the critics say, but to treat it as a problem of international security is an unwarranted distraction.

In India during the period 1996 to 1998, the birth ratio was 111 [boys] to 100 [girls].

Why Sons Are Preferred

The two political scientists began their project in the mid-1990s, when Ms. den Boer—who is now a lecturer in international politics at the University of Kent, in England—was a graduate student at Brigham Young. Ms. Hudson regularly assigned the philosopher Daniel Little's book *Understanding Peasant China: Case Studies in the Philosophy of Social Science*

(Yale University Press, 1989), which mentions that 19th-century Chinese rebellions were concentrated in areas that were disproportionately male.

Intrigued by that insight, Ms. Hudson and Ms. den Boer began to search for similar patterns elsewhere. "It was sort of random research at the beginning," says Ms. den Boer. "Where has female-selective infanticide been prevalent in the past? Then we looked at where the practice is prevalent today . . . and then looked further at the correlations with violence."

"I don't think we initially set out to write a book," she continues. "We initially, in fact, just wrote a conference paper. There was a lot of interest in that paper. The CIA [Central Intelligence Agency] came to the university and spoke with us about it, and wanted to know what United States policy should be toward countries that have this prevalence of infanticide and high sex ratios." (In demographers' jargon, a "high-sex-ratio" society is male-skewed, and a "low-sex-ratio" society is disproportionately female. The worldwide sex ratio is estimated to be 101, meaning that there are 101 men for every 100 women.)

Bare Branches offers some disheartening numbers: In 1993 and 1994, more than 121 boys were born in China for every 100 baby girls. (The normal ratio at birth is around 105 [boys for every 100 girls] for reasons debated among biologists, humans seem naturally to churn out slightly more boys than girls.) In India during the period 1996 to 1998, the birth ratio was 111 to 100; in Taiwan in 2000, it was 109.5. In 1990 a town near New Delhi reported a sex ratio at birth of 156.

Scholars have offered a number of explanations for the remarkable persistence of son-preference, which has lingered even in regions confronted by modernizing forces and government efforts to stamp out female infanticide. A powerful Chinese social norm, especially strong in rural areas, holds that sons must care for their parents in old age; people without sons thus fear poverty and neglect. In both India and China, various folk beliefs hold that only a son can perform the religious rituals that will ease a deceased parent's way into the afterlife.

Some scholars suggest that those norms and beliefs are remnants of a long-ago time when there were narrowly rational reasons to prefer sons to daughters. Anthropological studies have found, for example, that female infanticide and son-worship sometimes emerge in warring nomadic communities that frequently lose many men in battle, or that are vulnerable to having their women and children kidnapped by a rival group. In such situations, the theory goes, a group can preserve its integrity by tightly controlling the number of women within it.

Women Lack Power

Another theory holds that son-preference is a by-product of hypergyny, a system in which women are expected to marry men of higher social rank. Strongly hypergynous societies tend to have dowry rituals; the bride's family gives money to the groom's family as an emblem of the bride's subordinate status. (A Chinese truism says: "The family of the married daughter holds its head down, while the family of the man whom she has married holds its head up.") The great cost and social shame long associated with dowries can make parents cringe at the thought of having a new daughter.

Americans often assume that hypergyny and a preference for sons must be self-correcting, according to Ms. Hudson. As marriageable daughters become scarce, people will choose to produce more of them. Simple supply and demand, right?

"If there's an economist in the audience," the professor says, "he or she will raise this point: 'When you make something scarce, you'll make it more valuable—this will *improve* the social position of women.' And it's just utterly false. . . . It doesn't take account of the fact that the woman herself does not hold her value. That is, she herself could not use her scarcity to improve her condition, because her fate is determined by men, either her father or her husband's family. She herself cannot leverage her scarcity."

"There's also a sort of NIMBY phenomenon that goes on here," Ms. Hudson continues, alluding to the "not in my backyard" attitude. "Individual fathers and families will say, Yes, it's important that girls be born, that there be wives for our sons. But *I* want a son! We'll let somebody else have the girls."

Threats to Asian Stability

Whatever the causes of sex selection, Ms. Hudson and Ms. den Boer are certain that it threatens the stability of eastern Asia.

"We're right on the cusp," says Ms. Hudson. By that she means that birth ratios began to skew around 1985, as sex-selection technology spread, and that the "surplus" boys born in the late 1980s are just now reaching adulthood. "With every passing year, these surplus males will become more and more an important social factor." She cites news reports of spikes in drinking, gambling, and violent crime among young men in rural Indian villages.

As their ranks grow, these unmarried young men are likely to be attracted to militant organizations, the authors say. In such an "unstable context," they write, the conflicts over Taiwan and Kashmir, for example, are unlikely to be permanently settled. What's more, the governments of Asian nations may cope with the social strains caused by their "bare branches"—a Chinese term for men who cannot find spouses—by turning to militarism and ultranationalism.

"The security logic of high-sex-ratio societies predisposes nations to see some utility in interstate conflict," the authors write. "In addition to stimulating a steadier allegiance from bare branches, who are especially motivated by issues involving national pride and martial prowess, conflict is often an effective mechanism by which governments can send bare branches away from national population centers, possibly never to return."

> A series of empirical tests ... [demonstrate] a positive correlation between sex ratios and murder rates across India.

The authors rest their case in part on historical case studies. Female infanticide was rampant in 18th-century China, and the Qing dynasty responded by encouraging single men to colonize Taiwan, they write. As a result, Taiwan developed an extremely high sex ratio and soon was swept by groups that combined banditry with anti-imperial rebellion. The "Heaven and Earth Society" became so powerful that in 1787 the government was forced to send thousands of troops to restore order.

A similar story had unfolded in 16th-century Portugal, where primogeniture was in practice. Because first-born sons inherited everything, many later-born sons had no chance of finding wives. According to James L. Boone, a University of New Mexico anthropologist, such later-born sons banded together to persuade the monarch to launch wars of conquest in Africa. "It was above all *the cadets*," Mr. Boone wrote, "who lacked land and other sources of revenue within the country, who desired war, which would permit them to accede to a position of social and material independence."

Ms. Hudson and Ms. den Boer also point to a series of empirical tests—including one they have conducted themselves—demonstrating a positive correlation between sex ratios and murder rates across India.

Nothing in the two women's arguments, however, persuades Joshua S. Goldstein, a professor emeritus of international relations at George Washington University, who wrote *War and Gender: How Gender Shapes the War System and Vice*

Versa (Cambridge University Press, 2001). "The problem with their design is that they're basically just picking cases that fit their hypothesis, and so you don't know whether it's generalizable or not," he says. Mr. Goldstein would prefer a much more systematic study, one that would try to identify how sex ratios interact with other variables that are believed to be linked to instability and war: rapid population growth, ethnic tension, poverty, and unstable availability of resources.

Melvin Ember agrees. "Arguing by example is not anywhere near truth or confirmation," says Mr. Ember, president of the Human Relations Area Files, a repository of anthropological data at Yale University. "A better study would look at a large, randomly selected sample of societies with high, low, and normal sex ratios," he says. "It just requires a little bit of good will and money. The statistical techniques and the databases exist."

A similar complaint is offered by Manju Parikh, an associate professor of political science at the College of St. Benedict, who has written about offspring sex selection. "This is an example of social-science inductive reasoning, but it's not a very good example," she says. "They have to show why other explanations don't do as well. This is not a unique situation"—that is, she says, many countries with normal sex ratios have also been prone to instability and war.

Those complaints reflect a too-rigid model of explaining the world, responds Ms. Hudson, who teaches courses in social-science methodology. "This critique goes to the heart of how we know anything in the social sciences," she says, arguing that because skewed sex ratios are a still-emerging variable, it is appropriate to sketch their potential effects more loosely, using what she and Ms. den Boer call "confirmatory process tracing."

"I encourage others who wish to perform additional analysis using other methods to do so," Ms. Hudson says. "But until a question is even raised, it cannot be addressed."

Mr. Goldstein and Ms. Parikh also worry that the *Bare Branches* argument leans too heavily on what they regard as crude evolutionary models of male behavior. "The authors seem to completely lack empathy for these low-status rootless men," says Ms. Parikh. "These guys are the victims of development, and they call them criminals and potential criminals. This is so appalling." For instance, contrary to the book's suggestion, she says, most migrant workers in Asia maintain strong kinship ties with their home villages, send money home every month, and are nothing like the untethered marauders pictured in the authors' warnings.

Violent crime in the United States has been concentrated in areas with high sex ratios.

The term "surplus males," Mr. Goldstein says, "is offensive, and for lack of a better term, sexist. They're making a very conservative argument, which is sort of wrapped up in a feminist skin." It is a mistake, he says, to draw easy lessons from the finding that unmarried men tend to have higher testosterone levels than do their married peers.

Violence Is Documented

Ms. Hudson says she herself is skeptical of sociobiological explanations but finds it impossible to avoid engagement with them. "I don't know of any social-science findings that are more confirmed than the fact that young men monopolize violent antisocial behavior in every society," she says. "It may not be PC [politically correct] to say so, but you come up against such a mountain of evidence."

As for Ms. Parikh's point about migrant workers' kinship ties, Ms. Hudson says that "feeling kinship with home and village is not the point. . . . Even when bare branches stay close to home, when they congregate they form new systems of norms unto themselves." Those new norms are often aggressive and antisocial, she says. "Families cannot control their 'stakeless' sons."

Mr. Courtwright, of North Florida, agrees. His 1996 book argues that violent crime in the United States has been concentrated in areas with high sex ratios, like the old Western frontier, and areas with low sex ratios, like contemporary urban ghettos, from which significant numbers of men are "missing" because of imprisonment. Such demographic considerations should be central to any serious study of crime and disorder, he says. "Even if you don't buy their fears about war," he says of Ms. Hudson and Ms. den Boer, "certainly you can accept their predictions about crime and instability."

Organizations to Contact

The editors have compiled the following list of organizations concerned with the issues debated in this book. The descriptions are derived from materials provided by the organizations. All have publications or information available for interested readers. The list was compiled on the date of publication of the present volume; the information provided here may change. Be aware that many organizations take several weeks or longer to respond to inquiries, so allow as much time as possible.

American College of Obstetrics and Gynecology (ACOG)
409 Twelfth St. SW, PO Box 96920
Washington, DC   20090-6920
(202) 638-5577
Web site: www.acog.org

ACOG is the nation's leading group for professionals who provide health care to women. The organization advocates for quality health care for women, promotes patient education, and aims to increase awareness about women's health issues. Publications include the journal *Obstetrics & Gynecology,* bulletins, reports, and pamphlets.

American Society for Reproductive Medicine (ASRM)
1209 Montgomery Highway, Birmingham
Alabama   35216-2809
(205) 978-5000 • fax: (205) 978-5005
e-mail: asrm@asrm.org
Web site: www.asrm.org

The ASRM is a nonprofit organization that seeks to be a leading educator and advocate in the field of reproductive medicine. Articles about gender selection are available on the Web site. Publications include *ASRM News* and the journal *Fertility and Sterility.*

BetterHumans.com

Web site: www.betterhumans.com

BetterHumans.com is a Web site that advocates using science and technology to advance human progress. It supports gender-selection technologies.

Center for Bioethics and Human Dignity (CBHD)

2065 Half Day Rd., Deerfield, IL   60015
(847) 317-8180 • fax: (847) 317-8101
e-mail: info@cbhd.org
Web site: www.cbhd.org

CBHD is an international education center whose purpose is to offer Christian perspectives on bioethics issues. Its publications address sex selection and other reproductive technologies. The articles "Sex and Desire: The Role of Parental Aspiration in Sex Selection" and "Sex Selection Via 'Sperm-Sorting': A Morally Acceptable Option?" are available on its Web site.

Center for Genetics and Society

436 Fourteenth St., Suite 700, Oakland, CA   94612
(510) 625-0819 • fax: (510) 625-0874
e-mail: info@geneticsandsociety.org
Web site: www.geneticsandsociety.org

The center is a nonprofit organization that works to encourage genetic technologies that benefit society while opposing technologies that treat humans as commodities. It believes that sex selection can lead to problems such as violence against women and sex discrimination. The center works with health professionals and scientists to achieve its goals. It publishes annual reports and the newsletter *Genetic Crossroads*.

Council for Responsible Genetics (CRG)

5 Upland Rd., Suite 3, Cambridge, MA   02140
(617) 868-0870 • fax: (617) 491-5344
e-mail: crg@gene-watch.org
Web site: www.gene-watch.org

CRG is a national nonprofit organization of scientists, public health advocates, and others who promote a comprehensive public interest agenda for biotechnology. Its members work to raise public awareness about issues such as genetic discrimination and patenting life forms. CRG publishes *GeneWatch* magazine and has articles available on its Web site.

Hastings Center
21 Malcolm Gordon Rd., Garrison, NY   10524-4125
(845) 424-4040 • fax: (845) 424-4545
e-mail: mail@thehastingscenter.org
Web site: www.thehastingscenter.org

The Hastings Center is an independent research institute that explores the medical, ethical, and social ramifications of biomedical advances. The center publishes books, including *Reprogenetics*, the bimonthly *Hastings Center Report*, and the bimonthly newsletter *IRB: Ethics & Human Research*.

President's Council on Bioethics
1425 New York Ave. NW, Suite C100
Washington, DC   20005
(202) 296-4669
e-mail: info@bioethics.gov
Web site: www.bioethics.gov

The purpose of the President's Council on Bioethics is to govern the use of genetic information and protect the welfare of human research subjects. The council's Web site includes reports and transcripts on sex selection, including "Ethical Aspects of Sex Control."

United Nations Population Fund (UNFPA)
220 East 42nd St., New York, NY   10017
(212) 297-5000
Web site: www.unfpa.org

The UNFPA is an international development agency that promotes policies that ensure good health, safe pregnancies and births, and respect for girls and women. Gender selection is addressed in its publications, which includes the annual *State of the World Population*.

Bibliography

Books

Audrey R. Chapman and Mark S. Frankel, eds.
Designing Our Descendants: The Promises and Perils of Genetic Modification. Baltimore: Johns Hopkins University Press, 2003.

Celia Deane-Drummond and Bronislaw Szerszynski
Reordering Nature: Theology, Society, and the New Genetics. London: T&T Clark, 2003.

Susan Greenhalgh and Edwin A. Winckler
Governing China's Population: From Leninist to Neoliberal Politics. Stanford, CA: Stanford University Press, 2005.

Valerie M. Hudson and Andrea M. den Boer
Bare Branches: The Security Implications of Asia's Surplus Male Population. Cambridge, MA: MIT Press, 2004.

Richard T. Hull, ed.
Ethical Issues in the New Reproductive Technologies. New York: Prometheus Books, 2005.

Nie Jing-Bao
Behind the Silence: Chinese Voices on Abortion. Lanham, MD: Rowman & Littlefield, 2004.

Liza Mundy
Everything Conceivable: How Assisted Reproduction Is Changing Men, Women, and the World. New York: Alfred A. Knopf, 2007.

Maura A. Ryan — *Ethics and Economics of Assisted Reproduction: The Cost of Longing.* Washington, DC: Georgetown University Press, 2003.

Thomas A. Shannon, ed. — *Reprodu[ED1]ctive Technologies: A Reader.* Lanham, MD: Rowman & Littlefield, 2004.

Mary E. Shepherd — *Sex-Selective Abortion in India: The Impact on Child Mortality.* Youngstown, NY: Cambria, 2007.

Periodicals

Catholic New Times — "Sex-Selection Tests in India Mean Fewer Girls, Study Says," January 29, 2006.

Christianity Today — "Gender Is No Disease," February 2005.

Marcy Darnovsky — "Revisiting Sex Selection," *Genewatch,* January/February 2004.

Denise Grady — "Girl or Boy? As Fertility Technology Advances, So Does an Ethical Debate," *New York Times,* February 6, 2007.

A.C. Grayling — "The Power to Choose," *New Scientist,* April 9, 2005.

Ian Hunter — "India Turns the Corner," *Catholic Insight,* June 2007.

Issues and Controversies on File — "Gender Selection of Babies," May 13, 2005.

Claudia Kalb,   "Brave New Babies," *Newsweek*, Feb-
Barbie Nadeau,   ruary 2, 2004.
and Sarah Schafer

Felicia Lee   "Engineering More Sons than
                        Daughters: Will It Tip the Scales To-
                        ward War?" *New York Times*, July 3,
                        2004.

Neil Levy   "Against Sex Selection," *Southern
                        Medical Journal*, January 2007.

Mark O'Keefe   "Gender Choice: Is It Playing God?"
                        Christian Century, May 4, 2004.

Barbara Katz   "The Consequences of Sex Selection,"
Rothman   *Chronicle of Higher Education*, Febru-
                        ary 24, 2006.

Michael J. Sandel   "The Case Against Perfection," *The
                        Atlantic*, April 2004.

Katherine Selig-   "Chasing Chromosomes," *San Fran-
man   cisco Chronicle Magazine*, July 23,
                        2006.

Shirish S. Sheth   "Missing Female Births in India,"
                        Lancet, January 21, 2006.

Bijal Trivedi   "Boy or Girl? Embryo Tests Give Par-
                        ents the Choice," *New Scientist*, Sep-
                        tember 30, 2006.

Index

A

Abortion, 44–45
  China and, 69
  criminalizing, 31–32
  cultural factors, 74–75
  economic incentives, 36
  education and, 63–64
  feminism and, 75–76
  India and, 74
  late-term, 31–32
  rights, 31
  sex-selective, 9, 74
  South Carolina and, 31
"Abortion is Bad Karma: Hindu Perspectives" (Murti, Derr), 8
Access inequalities, 15
Adamson, David, 23
American College of Obstetricians and Gynecologists' Committee on Ethics, 50
American Society for Reproductive Medicine (ASRM), 13–14, 23, 25
Amniocentesis, 10–11
Annas, George, 25
Assisted reproductive technologies (ART), 10

B

Bare Branches: The Security Implication of Asia's Surplus Male Population (Boer, Hudson), 35, 54, 65, 78
Baruch, Susan, 23
Beijing Women's Conference, 75

British Human Fertilization and Embryology Authority, 19
Bush Administration (George W.), 73, 76

C

Caplan, Arthur, 24
Center for Bioethics, University of Pennsylvania, 24
Center for Reproductive Rights (CRR), 67
Child as gift *vs.* right, 20
China, 12, 28
  abortion in, 69
  birth control policies, 68
  family planning, 68
  female infanticide, 62, 83
  one-child policy, 15, 63
  prenatal diagnosis regulations, 70
  sex ratios, 15, 28, 38, 54–55, 61, 71, 74, 79–80
  traditional medicine, 69
Christianity, 7
Chronic villus sampling (CVS), 10–11
Civil rights, 36
Class issues, 15–16
Code of Ethics, National Association of Social Workers, 13–14
Commission on the Status of Women (CSW), 73
Conditional love, 47–48
Courtwright, David, 79, 86
CRR (Center for Reproductive Rights), 76